BABY
BOOMERS +

A guide to **designing these years,**
honoring the **full circle of life,**
and creating **life-giving conversations**

Dawn Sully Pile

Published by Dip Into the Well Publishing.

ISBN-13: 978-0692959268
ISBN-10: 0692959262

A NOTE ABOUT THE +

THE BABY BOOMER GENERATION IS currently the largest generation, comprised of approximately 76,000,000 Americans born between 1945 and 1964.

The original intention of adding the + was to include those born prior to 1945.

Through further reflection and in conversation, it became clear that the + also includes introducing this information into the minds and hearts of the children of Baby Boomers +, for whom there is a dedicated chapter.

Welcome to these pages, whether you are a Baby Boomer or a Baby Boomer +.

In the end, this book has a message for all adults.

DEDICATION

THIS BOOK IS FOR ALL who are of my generation, ahead of my generation, and after my generation.

May we give our children, loved ones, and friends . . . those who make up our family . . . the gift of conversation. It is about how we want to design our days and live now, how we want to honor the full circle of life, and that we choose to share pertinent information. It is about the big things and the often thought of little things such as our 100 passwords in cryptic cues, where the safe deposit box keys are or perhaps even the car keys!

May this book be one of your guides for navigating the journey with grace, joy, love and the determination to live each day as an adventure.

It is also in memory of and in honor of friends, whose lives changed so quickly that conversations and decisions had to be rushed while in shock or for whom there was not time. My moments with and about them are vivid and poignant. I write for them, too, and hold them in my heart.

TABLE OF CONTENTS

Part III

INVITATION

Bask in wild and
magical trust

A S I SIT HERE TO begin this book, staring out the window with the usual procrastination of choosing words to get me out the writing gate, I am noticing dozens of birds flying in what appears to be a haphazard pattern . . . circling in no order, diving down and swooping up, almost as if to create conscious distraction or chaos . . . round and round. Or perhaps they are simply romping on a Sunday morning with nothing holding them back.

My intuitional message of the birds, even in their total unawareness of my presence, is twofold.

The first intuition is about freedom and soaring. I want that for you as much as I want it for me.

The second is that the whole reason I deeply desire to write this book is to prevent chaos in families around knowing (or not knowing) what older adult family members want in their "third-third" of life. Order is a beautiful complement to freedom, and this book is designed to help you establish that, too.

This heart and soul book is your invitation to join me in the journey, one through which you will find yourself flying and soaring. Ultimately, you will settle in a place of grounded intention and capacity to fully embrace and communicate who it is you choose to be, and how, in the very best years of the "third-third" of life. And yes, all the way to your transition or passing, the full circle, the piece we tend to avoid talking about.

Each page is a beckoning to personal reflection and action that is uniquely yours. There is no single template to follow in these glorious years, so do not let anyone try to convince you otherwise. Step through the gate and into what is a field guide. Bask in wild and magical trust. You don't want to miss this!

INTRODUCTION

"If you ask me what I came
to this life to do, I will tell you.
I came to live out loud."

Émile Zola

SITTING IN A LAWN CHAIR circle, the gathering will always be embedded in my mind and heart. For as many qualities of my childhood family I am grateful for, communication was not a strong one or a modeled skill. So I recall this day of beautiful, intentional communication with love, respect and gratefulness. While I cannot tell you exactly what year it was, I am quite sure my parents were in their 80s at the time.

Our family gathered on the pavement in front of our barn rather than the usual sitting space on the grass. Perhaps the grass area was too shaded by that point in the day and we wanted to be in the sun and warmth, which I like to think of as light shining on the conversation.

A bit of mystery shrouded the "why" of gathering, as usual. Almost all calls for serious communication in my family held some charge, since deep and challenging topics were routinely absent except for during these rare requested times of convening. On a day-to-day basis, we did not argue or debate; conversation stayed above the surface where life would remain smooth and optimistic. The word and opinions of my parents were the word and opinions of my parents, with little room for discussion or changing their minds. At the same time, and connected closely to this work I am doing, they lived fully and in extremely positive mindsets. Age did not slow them down. I have often thought how beautiful it is that they did not get caught up in stories about aging that might have held them back. They lived according to what they wanted to do, not according to a number. That is a model I hold gently and passionately, a gift they likely did not even know they were giving me.

While I often wished and still wish that their set opinions and word had not been so set, I applaud that quality of their call for this particular conversation, which was to address their wishes for the end of life. Their desires, knowing, and resolve are exactly what I hope to possess in my own "third-third of life" conversations over the years to come, and a model for which I will advocate throughout this book.

INTRODUCTION

Of all the specifics my mother and father shared that day, the one that still stands out to me is their decision to donate their bodies to a medical center 90 miles north of our home so they could be part of contributing to research in any beneficial way possible. As a family, we had never shared so much as a whisper about that. When and where and how my parents even became aware of the option and when they made their decision remains unknown, yet they presented it to no argument from my brother, sister or me. In fact, it was not up for discussion, I'm sure.

I remember thinking then, as I do today, *what a beautiful choice.* Each of them had extraordinarily good health over their lifetimes and they felt if there was anything that could be discovered about the "why" of that, they wanted to contribute to others having long, healthy lives. My father lived to 91 and my mother, to 100.

Over the years and especially as I write this book, the gratitude I have for my parents' proactive, positive, clear conversation with us runs deep. For all the other conversations I might wish I had with them during their lifetime, I would not trade those for this ultimately most important one. They gave an extraordinary gift to our family that day in the afternoon sun, one that they delivered not with drama or sadness but in a grounded, practical way. They simply knew they needed to look ahead and have a plan, and they communicated their wishes clearly to us three.

I am particularly grateful that this was a face-to-face conversation. That, too, is what I want to model in this age of so much being communicated online. Being able to look into one another's faces, regardless of the potential for a variety of responses, brings a lasting memory that does not occur through words on a screen.

As a Baby Boomer, one of approximately 76,000,000 in the United States alone, I have a vision to provide not only a framework, but also lively conversation with other Baby Boomers + about how to talk with our families regarding how we desire to live what I think of as the "third-third of life," the years of 65 to 100 for me, and what we choose during our life's full circle. For "young" Baby Boomers, you have an extended time frame! This conversation encompasses not only end-of-life wishes, but also how to live these years in as robust and full ways as possible.

As I mention in the first pages of the book, I added + to Baby Boomers as many for whom this book and work is applicable are in the generation prior to 1945. I like + rather than "the silent generation" as is the title given to them. This book is about the opposite of silence.

You may be familiar with Simon Sinek's popular book, *Start with Why: How Great Leaders Inspire Everyone to Take Action.* I have thought long and hard about my WHY for this work and how I can lead this endeavor, hoping that it will be contagious the more people engage the conversation and work.

One essential WHY for this book is to ensure that families are spared having to traipse through the mire of lack of critical legal information needed after one's death. While this book is not about the legal documents per se, or the legality of anything pertaining to the end of life, it is about making sure that those crucial pieces of information are prepared, known, and available when the time comes. I have given more encouragement to this at the end of the book.

More joyfully, another WHY is to create open communication where older adults truly stand in their individual voices and declare—while in good health and clarity of mind—their choices for how to live. To dispel the notion that Baby Boomers + are in the beginning of a downhill slide or becoming "less than" they were in their younger years, I want to champion Baby Boomers + to create their personal "third-third of life" blueprint to affirm that the best is still to come.

Finally, a huge WHY is to celebrate and relish all that life holds in the "third-third" and to choose to live it fully and out loud. While the expression of "out loud" is unique for each person, it is rooted in living authentically and without apology. Most importantly, it implies not being swayed to make decisions that truly do not resonate and not being diminished by any "should" that others bring to the conversation. I think back to my parents and the clarity of their decisions, and feel grateful that they were able to communicate those without apology.

This work is about ordering our days to be fulfilling, exciting, rewarding, and at whatever pace we choose, from snail to speed demon.

So many conversations and readings have led me to this work, most of them about the extremely difficult circumstances families have found themselves in when lacking the knowledge of wishes and plans, living in the "too late now" space. If parents are still living but no longer capable of having these important talks, it brings added sadness and burdens to walking with them through their last years peacefully and gracefully.

It is easy to wonder why this even happens. Here's how I describe one of the typical reasons, perhaps the most common:

Tomorrow, tomorrow, there's always tomorrow . . .

Doesn't that say it all and bring an easy nod of the head (and maybe a guilty smile)? Of course. When I am with my daughter, there is so much more to talk about than my later years of life! Even when I intend to raise the topic, it no longer feels like the right moment . . . or . . . I'll wait until another day . . . or . . . or . . . or . . .

There are endless stories of families who wish their loved ones had not put off these important life-giving conversations. I call them "life-giving" because they present us ALL with a gracious opportunity to choose a positive approach and to experience a sustaining piece in the gift of connection.

In the "third –third of life," it is easy to let time slip by as we vacillate between the recognition of how important it is to communicate with family members about our desires for how we want to fully live out our lives and our hesitation to do so, leading to procrastination that too often leads to "too late."

NOW is the optimal time to step into a new paradigm. NOW IS THE TIME to free ourselves from hesitation, from worry about bringing up a "downer" topic, from procrastination and having the "should" hanging over our head. NOW IS THE TIME so that we can trade "tomorrow, tomorrow" for living with as much joyful abandon as possible.

While still of sound mind, with clear thinking and powerful intention—and before unexpected circumstances or emergencies intrude—NOW IS THE TIME.

By setting the bar and modeling how to thoughtfully choose to live fully no matter what our age, we leave a legacy for our children to model for their children and generations to come. It is a life-giving conversation in the family tapestry that starts a new thread.

I am so glad you are here, perhaps with a journal next to you so that you can personalize the content of this book and to explore how you can create, wrap, and give this gift of conversation to your family or those who are closest to you. It is an extraordinary blessing, a legacy, and in some ways a benediction that honors your life and theirs.

Step into it fully. Perhaps even dance into it with steps that are light, feet floating off the dance floor in the flow of the unique choreography of your life.

PART I

You
One of a kind design
No replacements
No duplicates
Genuine
Natural
You

YOUR PERSONAL "THIRD-THIRD OF LIFE" BLUEPRINT

"The urge for good design is the same as the urge to go on living (well*)."

Harry Bertola

*Author's addition

DESIGNING YOUR LIFE

F OR THIS MOMENT AND THIS time . . . if
you have not already done so.

In big or little ways.

Beginnings

"Growing up" has no age limits. We never "get
there." We are always growing up and I like to think
that we are growing like a tree, not simply straight
up but also with extended branches of beauty,
strength, and fullness.

Thinking back on the "what I want to be when I
grow up" answers I gave as a young person I
chuckle at the response I eventually settled on
decades later: "I'm still trying to decide what I want

to be when I grow up." How much do you resonate with that comment?

I wanted to be a nurse. I wanted to be a teacher. (You can tell my aspirations were heavily influenced by what women "could" be in the 50s). I also wanted to be a mother. I knew I wanted to help people. I wanted to be a singer and to perform in musicals. I wanted to play in a symphony orchestra. I wanted to be like famous women in biographies I read, to "be" Jane Adams or Helen Keller or to "be" a character from a book that captured my imagination and took me to all kinds of places that were incredible escapes, a favorite being "The Boxcar Children." I gave the "right" answers when asked, and they often depended on the moment and what was capturing my attention and imagination. In real life and for various reasons it did not feel like options were many, but in my world of dreams, the possibilities were endless.

So often, from an American cultural perspective, we are taught to plan our lives according to a path that goes in a straight line from childhood/youth to college or trade school to a job, even if we end up taking a more circuitous or personal route. The message has been conveyed from the beginning, from birth to college graduation, or perhaps going on for immediate advanced degrees: We need to "find a job." In some cases, this mandate is accompanied by additional words, like "make a good living" or "be successful."

I use the word "job" purposely, for that is how we so often frame the conversation. Growing up feels like it is ultimately with the goal to get the "right job" or to be in the "right place" or "make the right money and provide for _____." Reflecting back, there was a subtle message when teachers or relatives asked, "What do you think you want to be when you grow up?" It is very telling that this age-old question was not, and still often is not, "WHO do you think you want to be when you grow up?" but WHAT. As if the whole path needs to lead to the "what" and then all else will fall into place. WHO—our very being—was secondary to WHAT we were to become.

As I write this, I realize that we continue to perpetuate the same paradigm in many settings, even as we consider what to do in our older adult years. Shame on us, given our understanding of life and of "calling," and our knowing of that which is so much more beyond the black-and-white prescription. That is a topic for another writing. For those of us in our older years, we remember the prescribed expectations well. For those of us who had no idea, truly, *what* we deeply desired to do with our lives, it was a somewhat foggy road filled with "shoulds" and "if I don't . . ." and the oft-dreaded notion that we might not live up to what others expected of and hoped for us.

In many cases, we followed the steps and then spent the next 30-odd years fulfilling what felt like our defined and yes, even obedient responsibility. I use the word "obedient" because where we ended up often was not our choice but based on the recommendations or desires of others, and we never took the time (or were allowed the time) to reflect and choose. If we were extremely fortunate, we enjoyed our job and benefitted from it. Kudos to those who truly stopped to advocate for what they wanted, no matter what. In many cases, however, our stories begin with statements tinged with wistfulness or regret: "If I had only known then what I know now" or, "No one really stopped to ask me what I wanted to do . . . or who I wanted to be . . . I was expected to . . ." or, "If I could do it all over again, I would . . ."

My hope is that we abandon that pattern with children today and instill in them the knowing that they can follow their hearts, their passions, and their dreams to create the life they want from the very beginning, and that they can live each day in the authenticity of *who* they are at their core.

For those of you who are grandparents, I am visualizing as I write that you not only get to design your own life for the later years, but you also get to set the model for your grandchildren and their children, one that empowers them to live into their dreams even as you choose to live into yours right now.

Now

Whatever your past, it brought you to this moment, right here and now. You cannot go back and change anything that came before. The present moment is a time to be grateful for all that came before, no matter how magnificent or challenging or some combination thereof (which I am quite sure it was), because NOW is the time to step into full choice and full voice. NOW is the time to reclaim the dreams for everything that you ever wanted that has not yet happened. NOW is the time to say a resounding "yes" to immense possibilities, and to pursue all that you want to pursue and live into. The past does not need to dictate the future. You are in this moment. You are in NOW. We will come back to this and NOW will carry us.

Here is the story about my own coming to NOW. I would love for you to email me and tell me about yours: dawn@dawnsullypile.com.

I am a late bloomer. Some of you may have bloomed early on. Either way, we still are in choice about how to live the upcoming years and decades.

For my siblings and me, music was everything growing up. As the youngest of three I seemed to follow in their footsteps and we enjoyed camaraderie with this as a common interest. My brother inspired me to adopt the oboe as my instrument so as to be a bit different. Not many pursued oboe, with its double reed and absence from the marching band. He and my sister played more than one instrument. I became a proficient oboist, learning to craft all of my own reeds. In high school, I had the immense privilege of playing several concerts as the second chair oboist in The Hudson Valley Philharmonic. My teacher was the first chair oboist and when his colleague was out for a few concerts my teacher trusted me to fill in; I can still feel my pride and excitement.

I also played piano, though not as proficiently, and loved to sing. I joined every singing group possible during my school years. It seemed only natural at that time to me and to everyone else to go on to college to major in music, which I did. My freshman year in a conservatory, however, quickly showed me that compared to others from far and wide beyond my city, where I was considered a very good musician, I was nowhere near the best of the best. More importantly, I also discovered that I had neither the passion nor the dedication to make music my life. It was a pastime, a cherished hobby. Along with that awareness, I knew the field of music therapy, my interest, was waning at that time so I was left in a huge quandary. Knowing that I wanted to work closely with people, regardless of "job," I switched to sociology, a go-nowhere major in and of itself.

Fast-forward several years, in and out of minor jobs, married and with a child. I went to our Board of Education office to inquire about any possible job openings. It was on a total whim that I walked through those doors, lost in terms of what I wanted to do, and simply looking for a paying position. I walked out with the job of assistant teacher in a special needs class. Thus began 35 years in education . . . a field not on my radar screen except perhaps for the childhood answer of wanting to be a teacher. I had crossed that option off in college. But here I was, with no idea where that path was going to take me.

Education began as a "job" and along the way, over the 35-year span, callings wove themselves deeply into my work in ways I could not have predicted. Through those years, I moved from teaching into administration in independent schools. It was a livelihood that blended well with parenthood and was marked by invigorating and fulfilling connections with children and adults alike. There were many truly outstanding opportunities and experiences and I am grateful for my long career.

At the same time, I knew in a profound way that it was not the fullness of who I am. My passion was not the academic world, in which I felt I had failed miserably even as an avid learner of life. My passion, it became clear, was my mission to help children learn to value who they are and not compromise that, and to help parents parent in openness and authenticity rather than believing they had to follow a popular template or trend. It was also about mentoring faculty to teach through their strengths and through their leadership. I mentored them to learn to listen to the individuality of the children so they could see the nuances of who they really were rather than only seeing them through academic assessments. That's the short story. I grew exponentially and was fortunate to enjoy significant autonomy and trust most of the time. And when autonomy and trust was not extended, I was not my best. This is still true today, perhaps even more so.

Toward the end of that career I began to mull this step I am writing about: Designing MY Life. I knew, and had known for many years, that there was something else, whether it could be called "something more" or not . . . there was something else that I had not figured out yet that was calling me. Yes, *calling* me, beckoning, like a dormant seed waiting to encounter the right opportunity to grow. I'd been watching for it for decades.

During those years I pursued and completed my Master's in a program that was perfectly suited to me, a combination of theology, administration and counseling. This complemented all of my work and brought my little seed closer to the surface, but wasn't quite "it" yet.

Reading the newspaper one day—the kind that leaves ink on your fingertips—I found myself in the Business section, a section to which I rarely paid attention. One article stood out to me and I like to think it stood out FOR me, an article that changed my life. It was about a gentleman who had left the corporate world to become a coach. As I read I could feel, yes feel, not just think, that I was being led to a field I had been looking for all those years. As a result of emailing the gentleman, I found Coaches Training Institute. I immersed myself in the training, certification and soon after, Leadership Program. BAM! I knew I had, beyond a shadow of a doubt, found a major piece of my calling. I had been coaching others for years, even without the courses and certification. That was absolutely at the heart of my work, no matter who was in my presence or what my title.

Retiring from my education roles at 65 I embraced a whole new life and created my own hybrid coaching/consulting business with energy, imagination, and joy. I felt—and feel—that there is no stopping me, as I honor both semi-retirement and coaching, along with consulting, speaking, and writing in the other hours of my life. I see no end to it. I only see possibilities for continuing to live into and from my vision and mission.

Combined with this was the rediscovery of my passion for writing. Again, a knowing came to me: Instead of a musician, I was meant to be a writer. The boat of writers had sailed without me all those years; though I greatly enjoyed writing in a variety of themes and formats, I did not consider myself a writer. I do now. I have claimed "writer."

As a symbol of discovering what had been missing, what had been latent as a seed or seeds waiting to be watered, I gave my piano to a family whose children were taking lessons and needed one. It was as if I had to remove the piano from the house, clear that piece of my life, to fully step into writing. That sounds crazy, right? It may not be that way for everyone in the discovery process, and perhaps someday I will again have a piano. At the time it was a symbolic way of making room for my own transformation. As soon as the room was empty of that wonderful instrument, I felt like I was breathing fully; I knew that the pen was my true instrument.

This may seem like a long way to go about beckoning you to sink into designing your own life for these magical years; I share it as a testament to the fact that it can be done when we are open and do not place limits on ourselves.

Speaking of magical years, the term has often been used to describe the first few years of life. In fact, a 1959 book that became a classic is *The Magic Years: Understanding and Handling the Problems of Early Childhood* by Selma H. Fralberg.

I want to posit that these later decades in life are, indeed, the magic years . . . or perhaps to say that all years are the magic years . . . no decade or age has claim. This perspective creates a mind shift about aging and all of the false and unfortunate beliefs that are perpetuated. Shoo them off with the winds!

Here is what I want you to allow for yourself, knowing that a conversation with family is not meant to happen until you know who you are and how you want to live these decades, until your voice is full and certain and you are ready to share your own knowing with brilliant articulation.

Some ground rules, if I may:

- There is no right or wrong as you go through this process

- Stay open

- Live in curiosity and exploration

- Observe how you feel

- Let your heart and soul speak first

- As the saying goes, remember that if one door seems to close, another will open.

It is important to acknowledge that if you are part of a couple, it may be that you want to approach this in one of two ways. One, that each of you does the work separately and then comes together to share and blend your desires to design an awesome combination package. Two, that from the beginning you do this as a couple. However, it is important to realize that if one of you should end up being alone for a number of years, the optimal scenario is for each person to have at least an outline of his or her individual dream.

Diving In—Options Galore For You

This first piece of designing your own life is the most important. There is no instant answer or outcome, and it will call you forth magnificently to saying yes to digging deep, being honest, and even being willing to step into discomfort and courage as you choose to create the life you want. Perhaps you did that in the first fifty years of life. If you didn't, then now IS the time because we all know that there will not be another fifty years! And I promise you that each of these points will come in very handy as you consider how to have conversations with your family about your desires and choices.

I offer up design components (you are welcome to mix and match) as lights for your path to discovery. Feel free to add your own. You are the holder of more fabulous resources than you realize.

Included in the design process at this stage are also a couple of categories that I think of as important logistics that need to be secure so that the rest of life can be lived freely and fully. If you check them off, you will breathe more easily.

Practice, practice, practice

Everything from here on takes practice, so I urge you to allow that to happen without constantly critiquing yourself. When creating new perspectives and habits and stepping into ways of being that feel awkward or new and a bit unclear, know that practice is not only allowed but also encouraged. It makes all the difference.

I love the whole notion of practice and gained an entirely new perspective around it for my own life after reading a chapter in Natalie Goldberg's book, *The True Secret of Writing* titled *"What Is Practice?"* In fact, I am practicing writing this book . . . just practicing. I love it! It takes off so much pressure and angst.

Natalie Goldberg talks about this by looking at practice differently from the well-known phrase "practice makes perfect." She says:

It is something you do on a regular basis with no vision of an outcome; the aim is not improvement, not getting somewhere. You do it because you do it. You show up whether you want to or not.

Her whole point is that so often we talk about practice in order to get to a specific end point and that we can let that end point go. We get to practice for its own sake, for the joy of it, for the revelations of it, for a shift in our perspective. It builds confidence without a focus on a certain achievement. It is a fascinating discussion I wish I could personally have with all who are reading this book.

Allow yourself to practice . . . just practice what's here and see where it takes you. There is no judgment, simply practice. Notice how it eases everything.

Values

What is it that you cannot live without? Perhaps a better question is, "What are the most important things that anchor and steer your life?" Values can be tied to faith, morality, or ethics, but those are not the criteria. It really does come down to what anchors your life.

Let me share three of my values:

1. Morning Meditation

Sacred time and space as I begin my day is non-negotiable. I will get up as early as I need to in order to fit this in, even if a shortened version at times. It includes Silence, Affirmations, Visualization, Exercise, and Scribing (writing), or S.A.V.E.R.S as designed by Hal Elrod in his book, *The Miracle Morning*. Writing is a particularly strong value for me so even if I have to shorten other parts of the practice, writing never gets short-changed.

2. Connection

Connecting with people wherever I am is a high value of mine. Genuine connection, eye-to-eye connection, heart-to-heart connection, connections of all kinds depending on the moment and the place, connection just for the sake of connection, connection for business, service, or fun. Connection anchors me to who I am and why I'm here.

3. Serving

I derive great joy from serving others in myriad ways, always changing depending on spaces and circumstances in which I find myself and what else is taking place in my life. Sometimes serving another feels like a teeny tiny moment that might be huge for that person (and I might never even know) and at other times, is a bigger, more explicit project. My business is all about serving others, so serving is not necessarily tied to volunteering, a common false equivalency. From my very young years, I knew I wanted to be in work that serves others in some way, and so it has been and continues to be. Besides bringing a deep sense of joy, it just plain makes me happy.

This list can get you started thinking of your own. Values might flow seamlessly and seemingly endlessly as you begin to list them. Or you might find yourself puzzled and then realizing your values as you bump into them or they bump into you in interactions of all kinds. It may be that you discover that tenacity is a value, or patience, or justice; no matter what you discover, they are wholly yours. While they are open to change given the different circumstances of our lives, values are generally your guiding lights, your fixed stars. Be as specific as you can. If you are tempted to say, "being a good person," take time to unpack that a bit . . . what are the specific pieces or values of being a good person? How do you recognize it in action? What does it look and feel like?

Why knowing your values is so important is that when you live in resonance with them, when they are the markers, the benchmarks, the measures with which you connect all you are doing, you are likely to find yourself living a fulfilled, satisfied, and productive life. You will feel this in your core. There will be happiness and joy and you will see evidence of your values in living color.

When life is not aligned with your values, it feels murky, confusing, off kilter, and unsatisfying . . . perhaps not in all ways, but in enough ways that it calls you to stop and take an inventory to see where you have veered away from that which is most important, if not even non-negotiable and sacred.

Some questions for occasional reflection are, "Am I living in resonance or dissonance with my values?

What am I feeling? What am I experiencing? What am I hearing? What am I speaking out loud? What am I seeing as evidence in one way or another? Is there one that needs to be tweaked?" You will find your own ways to reflect and take stock as needed.

This is a foundational exercise I do with all of my clients and we come back to values as the touch point all the time. It is also informative to ask others what they observe or perceive as your values.

Choose your mindset

Mindset is everything. One of the best books I have read on this topic is *Mindset* by Carol Dweck. Published in 2006, it has gained a reputation for speaking to the power of our mindset and how we can consciously decide to live in a mindset of growth rather than a fixed mindset.

When we come to life with a fixed mindset, it is almost a given that "possibility" becomes a moot word or concept. "Fixed" and "possible" are rarely companions.

A growth mindset is ongoing, of evolution, of creating, of open-endedness . . . always with room for the new and unknown to enter and surprise us or be created by us. It is expansive. It energizes. It allows for imagination and trial and error and practice and discovery. It makes room for adaptation. It is limitless. It is filled with possibility and rewards us through the outcomes.

When I think of a fixed mindset I think of a small dark box, lid down, light not getting in, fear of anything different than what is known and believed, closed to exploration, and willing or even desiring to stay that way. Change, particularly significant change, is not an option to be explored.

It *feels* safe. But it is ultimately limiting.

If you realize that falling readily into a fixed mindset is your inclination, thank you for acknowledging that and deciding that these years are a perfect time to try on the growth mindset and see how it feels. I promise you will not want to go back once the adventures begin.

However, you may be naturally inclined already to as much expansiveness, change and growth as possible. If so, you will flow through this time in your life with ease. You will thrive.

A growth mindset allows you to "play full out." It makes me think of the time of young childhood when we played full out without knowing it . . . we just *did*. We got outside and ran around and chased and climbed and peddled without a care in the world and just kept going. We did not stop every 10 running steps to tell ourselves why it wasn't ok to do that; every ounce of our energy was spent on glorious freedom, movement, and tireless energy, often testing the limits of our capacities when we climbed high or gave it our all to cross monkey bars. There was no stopping us.

How many times as adults do we say, "Oh to have the freedom of childhood again."

You can. It is all about mindset, no matter what the circumstances.

Create solid intentions

Creating intentions is one of the most wonderful of life's discoveries for how to engage with what we want. Without intentions, how we approach our days and years can be fairly willy-nilly, "whatever," and often lacking responsibility.

Intentions can be set for the tiniest of things all the way to the most enormous shifts and decisions. It is rather startling how having a big, solid intention for what seems like a tiny thing makes all the difference in the world. One of my intentions for this book is "I will write so that my words will best serve the reader."

Intentions are focus, clear focus. It is not that they do not get revised or revisited, and they may even show up for a particular reason on one day. When I am writing an intention down I feel like I am looking through 20/20 vision with no smudges. There is a sense of knowing what is needed and desired in articulating an intention.

Intention is a declaration with purpose. It often has an envisioned outcome. We know that to get to that outcome it is imperative to set an intention or perhaps more than one.

Intention can be "easy" or it can be bold and significant. Intentions come in all shapes and sizes; however, they are serious, not frivolous, and are meant to generate action, guide, and help us aim and hit the target. They are made in the spirit of getting where we want to go, being who we want to be, and creating what we want to create.

Intentions also pair with willpower. It is one thing to be absolutely intentional about writing down an intention, and another altogether to *remember* it when you go to the next room or are caught up in life's details days or weeks later. I know whereof I speak! To this end, not only do I write daily intentions on a card, but I also carry the card around with me (at least that is my intention!). The card becomes a checkpoint, reminding me to pause when I am about to decide to do something that is totally not in the game plan. The card, in its own way says, "Stay with me. Remember your intentions."

Intentions can relate to what you want to get done or they can, on a deeper level, be significant in *how* you want to be, with yourself, with others, or in certain situations. As I was writing this section I stopped to email a friend who called me earlier about needing to have a challenging meeting at her child's school. It occurred to me as I sat here writing about intentions that this is a prime moment for her to create specific intentions for the conversation that needs to be had. There are endless opportunities for clear intentions. Start with choosing one or two main areas where you'd like to try them out. There will be more about intentions in a later chapter.

Open Studio – Blank Canvas – Empty Pages – Construction Supplies – Open Mind and Heart

For years, I have held an image in my mind of a studio I will have someday—yes, I am counting on it. It is a large room with huge windows that look out over green space with an expanse of water beyond. Light pours in. An enormous rustic but smooth table sits in the middle. A huge easel and blank canvas are over to the side and one complete wall is whiteboard paint for mind mapping. A warm gentle breeze wafts through and seems to bless the creative process and the space.

My life, too, and yours, is a canvas . . . or a book with hundreds of blank pages yet to be written . . . or a construction project of its own design . . . all with a mind and heart that are open and spacious, inviting of inspiration and expectant. They only expand, never contract, when it comes to designing a life.

Too often when we are in a place of "what's next?" we don't dare to let ourselves step outside the imprints of limitations that have invaded or are embedded in our minds and hearts. We have walls up or live in boxes of limitations that we allow to confine us. It is only when we can see our life as a blank canvas or one of the other visuals (and please, create a spacious one that fits you if none of these do) on which we get to be in full choice. We can step into full imagination and intention to design a fulfilling life, and then—beyond the dream stage—we get to make it real. We get to make the painting come off the canvas, the book that tells the story is being made real, and the construction is coming to life with movement and unbridled energy.

It is a full life when in alignment with values. It is a life that comes from purpose and passion.

It is never, never too late to be open to designing your life. It means stepping into choice, moving beyond fear, claiming your full voice, committing to action steps, and beginning. One brush stroke on the canvas with a favorite color, choosing what the next paragraph of your life will be, constructing a new doorway or window or gate . . . however you and you alone want to create your minutes, hours, days and years.

Allow your design to evolve in and through an open and invitational spirit. Notice when it truly shows up and experience the thrill of saying yes.

Hint: Looking back to childhood

Jenifer Fox, in her book, *Your Child's Strengths: Discover Them, Develop Them, Use Them,* notes at some point that so often our strengths show up in relatively early childhood years and too often are not noticed or perhaps not acknowledged, for lots of different reasons. I am not going to go into that here, but it is important is to realize that if we look back at our childhood, there is often an "aha" moment of realizing, beyond the "right answers," that what we have wanted to do all these years was rooted there. It was a dream . . . it was a hope . . . it was, in fact, so much a part of who we are at our core.

However, this knowing got covered up or put aside or someone had other ideas for us. Take a moment and see if there is any resonance in this for you as you consider how you want to design your "third-third" of life. Now is your chance. There is definitely some way that you can connect to and embody that core desire, intuition, knowing, or dream. Ask yourself how it might still be possible to bring this neglected but newly recognized piece into your life in some way.

Visualize

Visualization is one of the most powerful tools I use. I know, I know, for some of the Baby Boomer + generation it drums up "new age" and woo-woo (a fixed mindset perhaps?). I am asking you to set those perspectives off to the side or put them out to pasture, and to allow for the exceptional ways visualization can change your life.

A pertinent example as my fingers glide across the keys is this: As I think of speaking to Baby Boomers + on the topic of how to have intentional "third-third of life" conversations with family, I visualize standing in front of everyone with this book in my hand, excited to share it, confident that it is going to open hearts and minds. I visualize inscribing copies for attendees and orders flowing in even when I am sleeping. I visualize people having aha moments—literally choosing a face of someone and seeing the joy. I visualize my own joy and the huge satisfaction I take in having completed a cherished project.

That, my friends, is not woo-woo at all. It is exhilarating. And it inspires me to keep typing and to set strong intentions for one of my dreams to come true.

The truth is that we all visualize every day, and we even visualize what we secretly want but are afraid to share. We visualize what we will look like at a certain weight or in certain clothing or in a car of our dreams. We visualize full bank accounts. Sometimes our dreams are subconscious visualizations. Visualization is part of our life . . . no denying it. What if we put this to purposeful, magnificent use to bring to life that which we truly and even deeply desire in myriad ways?

It can be as simple as taking five or ten minutes every morning to engage in quiet visualization, seeing specifically what you want to be your reality as your reality.

Another popular method of visualizing is creating a vision board. Find pictures and words that represent what you desire, whether it's something you want to own or an environment in which you want to live, a way of being you hope to develop or a whole new profession. The vision board, when posted, becomes a touch point to remind and pull you back to seeing yourself in it . . . as if it is *right now*. It is not up to me to say what is right for your vision board or how "out there" is ok. It's all yours! Go for it! Have fun with it and let yourself believe in the power of visualizing as playing a prominent role in where you find yourself in the future.

Listen to your intuition

How many times in our life have we uttered the words, "If I had only listened to my intuition . . ." and then convey the stories that follow? Conversely, and thankfully, there are just as many stories when intuition led the way and the outcome was remarkable. Life without attending to and welcoming our intuition brings regret; letting intuition be our guide allows us to see its brilliance and at times, its protection.

I remember reading somewhere that intuition is seeing with an inner eye. I love that. It is as if something very precious is working on my behalf, pulling my attention to an important inward knowing, observation, or light that wants to be recognized and heeded.

I also think of intuition as a soul message. It does not come from my brain, though the brain also has its moments. In fact, my brain sometimes works overtime wanting to close intuition down. When I pay attention to intuition and don't shut it off, it frequently, in fact, saves me from my brain. It would love for me to put the word "regularly" in there, too . . . practice, practice!

Think of a time when intuition came as a feeling . . . viscerally, physically. Or showed up unexpectedly and in exactly the right moment.

At times, intuition seems mysterious and perhaps feels like a sneaky little thing; at others, it is as clear as can be to the point that there is no possibility of ignoring it.

So what is the key? We know we have intuition. We also know it is there for our good. There are books written about it and the crucial role it plays and yet we often struggle to accept it as a part of who we are. We treat it like an outsider and ignore or doubt its validity.

Two key ingredients come to mind:

1. TRUST

How many times does it take for intuition to show its spectacular purpose in our life before it proves itself and earns our undivided attention and trust? When might the day come that the second we "hear" it or feel it we say yes to it . . . "Yes, you take the lead, intuition, please." How many times after a particular incident where it has shown up and we vow we will never distrust it again do we fall back into the old pattern of our brain leading?

It may be that you have mastered listening to your intuition. I believe there are people who have, and who consider it one of their richest traits. They have crossed the threshold of doubt that nudges when intuition shows up and without hesitation follow and trust the intuitive messages.

There is not much more to say. It requires practicing TRUST, living in trust, and knowing that the majority of the time trusting our intuition will take us in a wise direction. It is giving intuition the credibility it deserves and longs for. It is there waiting to lead, happy to lead.

2. LISTENING AND FOLLOWING

Hand in hand with the trust are the agreement and willingness to listen and follow . . . to act on and with our intuition. Period. That's it.

Yes, there may be times when we think we were hearing and following our intuition and everything went awry. It can happen. I believe, though, that the more we learn how to attune to our intuition versus our brain tricking us into thinking we are hearing our intuition (because the brain will soon disprove itself as dependable that way except on occasion), the more we will know. There are no hard and fast indicators that I know of to spell out. It is leaning into it and learning to notice the difference of what is true and when an imposter is speaking to us wearing an intuition costume.

When listening, we have every right to sit with it if there is no immediate emergency. Explore it and see what shows up. I often ask clients, "What is your intuition?" Another, less mystical, way of asking this is, "What is your gut telling you?" At times, we literally feel the truth or the right action in our gut.

Don't be hesitant to say, "Thank you, intuition" when it is especially needed and shows up magnificently.

What you want less of in your life . . . or do not want at all. What is it time to let go of?

What I find as I coach my clients is that the answers to this question spill out freely, sometimes without my even asking. If I do ask, the floodgates open for the answer or answers to be expressed and heard. Sometimes, it is the first time a client has allowed these to be spoken out loud even if they have been rolling around inside or coming to a boil.

Here is a great place to insert a valuable tip, one that has no expiration date.

Know that when you declare what you "want less of" it is rarely with a stopping point at the end of the list. The next word you are apt to find yourself saying is, "BUT . . ." It is so easy to list the rationale for why you have not yet taken this step and find yourself allowing these "things" to reel you back to them. Perhaps you feel someone in the family will be offended or that you will feel lost or in unfamiliar territory as you create new paradigms for living. On occasion it means letting go of a relationship that is not serving you, a challenging step. Realize that you can (and sometimes it takes gumption and fortitude) unhook "it" from the reel and let it go. You can reframe your perspectives and experience the freedom that comes with the release.

Here is the KEY WORD to replace "but . . ." that you want to immediately put into your expression of what you no longer want or what no longer serves you and may even be toxic. Ready for it?

AND.

I'll offer a quick example and then I have no doubt that your own examples will come fast and furiously.

"I no longer want to be so engaged in social media and the way it steals time from other things that are important to me, BUT I am afraid my friends will think I don't care about what they post and also that I will miss important news."

Reframe:

"I no longer want to be so engaged in social media and the way it steals time from other things that are more important to me, AND I am going to let my friends know that while I care about what is happening in their lives and value their friendships as much as ever, I have made a decision to spend less time on all social media and put the time into interests I am passionate about delving into and developing more fully. I know I cannot do both so I will still check in on social media and also let myself be free, with no guilt, knowing that I am choosing to step into what I want more of in my life."

Yes, the "and" answer might be longer because we often need to process the choice instead of staying in the "but." This all-powerful shift to "and" ushers us across the threshold into new resolve.

Decide what it is that you want less of in your life . . . AND . . . claim it. Take an action that will make it so.

I can almost hear the sighs of relief. You're welcome!

What you want more of in your life

Ahhhh . . . here comes the easy part . . . or not!

Imagining what you want more of in your life might be incredibly easy. It also does not mean that there are not new and perhaps even disconcerting action steps to make this list happen, AND it is exhilarating to listen to what it is you truly want.

It does not mean there will not be compromise or a waiting period for answers or answers that look different and ultimately surprise you because they are so much better than you imagined. This ties in closely with visualization.

In numerous conversations, again, mostly with clients, when I ask, "What do you want more of in your life?" or they address that question on the questionnaire I send them, the answer is "I don't know." Not always, but often. Or there is one idea and then they get stuck.

Often, this is because of still living in the "what I want less of" mode and being so stuck there that they can't imagine life differently. They do not know how to or how to allow themselves to dream. It is so easy to be caught up in the "what I want less of" that we forget the other side of this equation.

Here is a suggestion for bringing this to reality, so that you don't just nod your head about this and then skip to the next part.

Tips for exploring the question, "What do you want more of in your life?":

- Create two columns. Write your "less of" list in one column. Flip it to the "more of" in the opposite column.

- If this exercise feels challenging, allow the doors of your imagination to open, even a crack. Give yourself permission to be in what you want, desire, choose . . . or even just to sit and daydream and see what comes to you.

- Write down what you hear and feel free to write it hundreds of times. I have certainly done that. I have written the same thing literally hundreds of times in journals.

- Visualize what you want moving towards you in space. Take time each day to see it happening, see yourself in it, see it arriving, whatever that is. If thoughts come that want to argue, let them go in and out of your brain and then go back to your heart as you continue to visualize the manifestation.

- If you relish approaching this artistically, create a vision board, per the earlier section. With that visual your desires show up in your clear sight line each day. Or write a poem or a song or choreograph the dance you will dance and to what music. Instead of feeling silly or woo-woo, agree to play full out in stepping toward what is coming to you.

- Do not give up and do not settle for less. I cannot tell you how tempting this will be in some moments, or even days. Stay. Stay in your vision.

For those of you who might need this caveat, even though I fully support dreaming bigger than big, I am not suggesting that if you want five million dollars you look for it to arrive tomorrow or if you want a new home you wait for someone to walk up to the door of your current one and offer to buy it. We are called to *act* toward receiving what it is that we want. This is not about automatic magic, rabbits-out-of-a-hat stuff. It's about real, authentic, deep desires for which we are willing to work our tails off, whatever that means, to bring them into our lives AND trust that they will come in the right timing. Yes, TRUST. Maybe something even BETTER will show up. That is exactly the moment we are often surprised!

Geography and Home

This is a very simple category, or perhaps short is a more appropriate word.

Where do you want to live during these years? What are the qualities of that place? Yup! A little bit more of "what do you want? What are you choosing in spite of what others, more specifically, family members, might prefer?"

Health and wellness

Speaking of steps . . . as you design your life for this "third-third," how do you describe your current health? That is a holistic question.

Here is why I am asking, mincing no thoughts.

I want you to LOVE, LOVE, LOVE these years!!! I sure intend to, and I want Baby Boomers + around the world to join me in proclaiming that they are the best. It may be that your life up until now has been "best" already . . . in which case, I want that to continue for you. That includes health and wellness in all realms: Physical, emotional, mental and for many, spiritual.

Our culture, whether meaning to be humorous or serious, has played a significant role in rolling out messages that give negative labels to various ages. We're warned about the terrible twos . . . watch out for adolescence . . . the invincible 20s . . . black bands for 40 . . . and after that it gets into "over the hill" for almost everything from 50 on. I have resisted them all, even as I resist many other labels in life.

As they say, there is always truth in humor or maybe it is that humor somehow plants a seed making us expect the worst. Countless people I know speak about aging with regret even though it has not happened yet. The anticipation may literally be killing them.

Not only that, but every little thing that happens is excused (HUGE excuses!) to aging and sometimes we have to go buy a new bright red Corvette to pretend it is not so. Changes happen as we age that are going to happen. Wrinkles develop, no matter how small, and gray hairs begin to show, no matter how few. Yes, not necessarily and not that they must, but some body parts such as hips, which have been mightily engaged over the years, begin to ache. They do. Over our lifetime we lost "baby fat" and teeth and were prone to acne. We rarely, to never, look like what we think of as "perfect." There are simply some body development markers that go with the continuum of life. I, for one—even when inclined to pull back my developing or beginning to sag jowls that remind me of how "old" my relatives seemed when I was in junior high, realizing I am now them—love the wisdom that comes with wrinkles. I see gorgeous wrinkled faces that make me want to sit down with a cup of tea to see what I can glean from that person. And now, I hope I am becoming that person someone wants to sit down with and glean from me any wisdom I might have to offer.

Aging is beautiful in new and refreshing ways. We get to choose activities and habits that will make us stronger, to push our bodies and minds beyond what we think they can take—and it is being proven that they can become stronger. While writing, I read about the 94-year-old woman who broke the world's record for the oldest person to complete a half marathon, and several years before that she set the record for the oldest person to complete a marathon, having started running in her 70s.

Lest you not be inspired enough by this first example, I am also in awe of Sister Madonna Buder, a nun who at the age of 86 was still competing in triathlons. Her first triathlon was in 1985 at age 65. She completed 40 Ironman races in 30 years.

As I share these examples I do not do so with naiveté. I do not at all dismiss illnesses and conditions that occur that are challenging, and mean a different lifestyle or actions, conditions that do not allow us all to be triathletes. They can take us by surprise at any time on the life continuum. However, while I want to be sure I say that and recognize it, I also believe that we are not innocent in having brought some of the illnesses to ourselves, which is why I am so vocal in this section about choice and *not assuming that age will mean deterioration.* Yes, there are some genetic dispositions; there are also new arguments about mindsets around that. I am not an expert in that arena so will not say anything more.

I am convinced, however, that mindset, attitude and conscious choices are enormous. To quote Sister Buder, "You carry your attitude with you. You either achieve or you self-destruct. If you think positively, you can turn even a negative into a positive. I realized the only failure is not to try, because your effort in itself is a success."

Please, I implore you, do not give into using progressing age as an excuse if that is the truth of what you find yourself doing. I am speaking to not allowing ourselves to "go to pot" as I used to hear when I was a child because we think it is a badge of age. I am speaking to not eating more and more healthily, not giving our bodies the exercise they not only need but can thrive on more than we think (so many videos to prove it if proof is needed), to not becoming couch potatoes or continuing to be couch potatoes when it will only lead to mental, physical, and emotional atrophy if that becomes our *modus operandi*.

Choose health. Choose wellness. Choose the best habits in this area you have ever chosen. They can be transformative. Choose to look into natural health so your body stays clear of as many toxins as possible.

I choose organic as often as I can. I choose to use essential oils as they are proving to have amazing effects on so many aspects of our overall health and wellness. I choose to walk almost every day and use weights and sometimes I pay for classes to keep me going and sometimes I am good on my own. I choose to read up on new research and information that will keep me healthy to 100. I chose to switch from conventional medicine to a functional doctor who knows conventional medicine and integrates natural healing. Every one of these is a powerful choice *for me*.

My parents were excellent role models. Everything was in moderation. No one ever sat with a bag of chips by their side and an evening snack was as often a bowl of mixed citrus fruit as anything else. If my dad enjoyed chocolate, he took an old Skippy Peanut Butter cover and put only as many Nestle chocolate chips in it as would cover the bottom and did not go back for more. Serving sizes and dish sizes were far less and we were never hungry. My parents took care of a home and 10 acres with no help. I have often said that in those days there were no such things as health and exercise clubs because we mowed the lawn by hand, hung out the washing and brought it in again, raked the leaves, shoveled the snow and bodies were on the go all the time. There were few to no preservatives in any food so whole milk with cream on top was pure and without antibiotics or GMOs.

Looking at sets of dishes from even the 1970s (much less the earlier decades) in comparison to now, it is clear that the size of a cereal bowl or dinner plate or coffee/tea cup have all grown as what are considered "normal" portion sizes have grown. It is as if we inched our way to bigger and bigger without realizing how much the impact slows us down physically. The rates of diabetes and heart disease have increased exponentially in our country. My goal is to not get into a debate but simply to offer up that each one of us has the power to make choices. A quote posted in my kitchen says, "You will eat according to who you BELIEVE yourself to be"—and it makes me pause and reflect each time I read it.

We are always in choice and when we choose the best health possible by building and maintaining great health habits, life is far more energized. As long as it is in my power, I will keep moving and doing all I know to stay well. I hope that in this you will join me. For those of you who already thrive in these patterns, kudos!!! Share your success habits and stories! Be contagious!

Play!

Here is another short one. I almost took this section out. I am choosing to leave it, though, because how we engage our time in pleasurable activities makes a difference. Not only that, but when we try new things we might find we have discovered a new passion or a gift we did not know we have—or just plain fun!

I have recently been following the joy of a woman who is dabbling in painting and I can almost feel her glee coming through the screen as she tries various brushes, colors and texture, and creates unique designs. Her smile is contagious and makes me want to pick up paints to see what I, too, might discover. She has rearranged her house to accommodate this new delight.

I want to insert a recommendation here and that is to read Stuart Brown's book, *Play: How It Shapes the Brain, Opens the Imagination, and Invigorates the Soul.* It is a book for all ages and if all ages adopt it, what fun can be had across generations together.

Indulge! Discover! Make the time! Freshen up your gifts! Play!

Animals

If you love them, animals are such great companions.

Have as many pets as you want and that bring delight to you. Be sure to build into your will, as well as possible future plans should you have to move to a new place where you cannot have pets, how they will be taken care of. This is no different than parents having plans for who will care for their children in case of emergencies. Indeed, we often talk about our pets as our children in later years. They deserve our attentiveness in having back-up plans even when we hope those will not be needed.

A well articulated and agreed upon plan allows a huge measure of grateful relief from worry so pets can be totally enjoyed, spoiled, and provided for.

I made a significant geographical and life move during the writing of this book. Without a pet in my new home I made friends with Annie, the miniature goldendoodle who lives downstairs. She now has a dog bed in my apartment and when she bounds up the back steps to spend time with me I feel the energy quotient in my apartment skyrocket . . . well, it is the energy quotient in me that does that. She also has a contagious effect when it comes to joy and she reminds me that a furry creature brings the most wonderful life to living spaces. It is obvious, when seeing the impact of animals visiting in assisted living homes or with those who are gravely ill, that they uplift and connect and even bring their own version of healing moments. I dare say animals' souls connect with ours.

Legal documents all created / checked off!

I have no law background at all. None of my work is about the legal side of life; however, as part of my work I advocate for all Baby Boomers + to make sure that everything needed from a legal standpoint is completed and either shared openly or that family members are given the necessary contacts for when the time comes.

It is all too easy to put off having all documents completed and current. This is often one of the last responsibilities people want to attend to as it makes the reality of our passing from this lifetime more real than perhaps we desire. It might bring up stories from your own parents and what was prepared or not. You might wrestle with how to approach dividing up your possessions and assets, or making health decisions when they still seem so far off. Perhaps you're just used to being in the mode of "tomorrow, tomorrow."

My strong encouragement to you is that this is as crucial a part of your life blueprint for the "third-third of life" as anything. As you take the step to complete all vital documents that will save untold red tape, frustration, and potentially significant hurt and loss, spend some time creating and writing down strong, purposeful intentions for the task. Incorporate your values and know the gift you are giving in taking care of these matters.

It is fully possible to engage in the path of completion of the legal details with joy and with deep care rather than drudgery or whatever challenging emotions and thoughts might arise for you. It could be that this challenges you to actually declare what you want. Great! I love putting that challenge out there because as I have said before, "NOW is the time." Live in the vision of paving a smooth path for closure when it arrives.

If helpful, consider meeting with an estate or eldercare attorney to make sure that nothing is missing in what will best suit your individual circumstances.

This is a great one to be able to say, "Check!"

Clearing away any fog

Recently I received happy, exuberant, loving kisses via licks to my face from Annie . . . the tongue not only touching my nose but also extending up to my glasses. All in love, affection, the full intention of letting me know I am loved and not realizing the lenses of my glasses were getting "fogged up." That's the kind way of putting it. The very first thing I did on getting into my house was to spray and clean the lenses. I know I know . . . some of you think I should have washed my face first but I don't mind dog kisses! I do, however, want to be able to see clearly. Over the span of our growing up years, so many people enter our lives with all good intentions, wanting the best for us, showering us with "kisses" of ideas and directions and assessments, suggestions for how they feel we "should" and "could" be, and so much more. This is really its own book . . . but let me simply say that for reasons we are trained in early, we too often have allowed the lenses of our life to be fogged up by others so that we are not seeing clearly, we are not hearing clearly, and we are not choosing clearly. We are, instead, often following because we have not been trained to find our own way, hear and trust our own voice, and see with our own mind and heart. Most of the time it is because everyone else has such genuine intentions for us from *their* point of view. The emphasis on "their" is important to acknowledge.

If that has been your story (and if not, you can skip this section), now is the time to clean your own lenses, to spray off what keeps you following others or not seeing clearly for yourself, and choose to clear and clean and make your own path. No more following. That is not to say that mentors and coaches and others, even children, do not serve a purpose in your life as you choose your own steps . . . but your choice comes FIRST. You are the one to choose who lends influence and inspiration that will help you reach your desired way of living.

Being in choice and living our choice is vital to health and wellbeing. I cannot emphasize enough, especially as you move into conversations with family members about your desires and choices, that you do this cleaning and clearing first so that you will stand in your voice. It may mean letting others know that you while you appreciate the love behind their intentions and opinions, you are clear about your choices.

The clearing/cleaning process is just that. Little specks and sometimes big spots smudge our life lenses, and we get to clean them off, to stay in our clarity. It makes me think of the song, "On a Clear Day" by Barbara Streisand.

On a clear day
Rise and look around you
And you see who you are
On a clear day
How it will astound you

That the glow of your being
Outshines every star
You'll feel part of
Every mountain, sea and shore
You can hear from far and near
A world you've never heard before
And on a clear day
On that clear day
You can see forever, and ever, and ever
And ever more.

Gremlins and Saboteurs

They are alive and well!

I want to speak to blocks that may well come up along the way, and that try to get you to stall or abandon your resolve. Let's get them out of the way as part of the clearing, so that your design stays alive and well and thrives.

In coaching, there are various terms: The gremlins, the saboteurs, the voices in your head or on your shoulder, or simply your learned perceptions of reality that automatically cancel out the ability to have what you want. Let me give you two examples of how these voices show up.

"I Told You So" is a tiny little nuisance of a girl that shows up in my world far too often. She is so, so tiny and has the ability to dart anywhere so that I can't see her but her voice is like a pipe organ with all the stops out. She creates havoc and loves doing so. The minute, or even second that a piece of my dreams or intentions or actions contains a wrinkle that needs to be ironed out, out pops her voice. She has the most annoying, frustrating, uncanny way of deflating me and taking me back and back and back through all failings, even though I know so well that what are perceived as failings/failures lead to something better. She, however, does not believe that and does not want *me* to believe that, so at exactly the moment I hit a small bump or challenge, she sees her role as "I told you so . . . I told you that you won't _____ so just give it up now . . . you're done . . . this is obviously not going to work" and on and on and on. As I write this book she is as active as ever. I am getting more skilled at a shorter response time, sending her to "I Told You So" 24-hour play facility to be with others like her and leave me alone. Silencing her takes diligence, an immediate "Nope . . . you are not allowed here today," and a commitment to my goals.

Another voice, and I share this with all love for her, is my mother's. There is not one iota of doubt of her love for me. It was out of love and the best motives that she spoke her disappointment, couched as encouragement, in ways that I have been working out of my life for decades, mainly in one area of my life: Academic grades. I am not a test taker. I am a doer. I am a speaker. I am a creator. I am someone who sees things with different perspectives than many. I struggle to recall details. I often did not read a whole sentence before answering a question on a test or doubted my intuition so went with a wrong answer. All of that led to grades below my known IQ and her hopes and her belief that I could do so much better. "You could be valedictorian like _____." "You need to try harder." She was parenting in the best way she knew how. Unfortunately, those were the days before understanding learning and the brain. I was not understood as a learner, nor were there options that would reveal what I knew or where my strengths did come to the fore. False assumptions were made, and I can recall moments of wanting to scream, "You have no idea how hard I have tried." Good motives resulted in damaging long-term messages. Believe me, there was enough self-criticism to last a lifetime and that, too, is a saboteur. I have worked very hard and diligently to erase this voice, to eradicate its power, and to choose, instead, to hear my mother's voice when it was acknowledging, encouraging, or filled with humor. Most importantly, I can say I have created peace with it.

Be willing to recognize the saboteurs and gremlins in your life and make a conscious decision that they will no longer be given power . . . that they have ZERO power. That's right: ZERO. Learn to dismiss them the second they show up because when we give them any credibility or time they cling and take the lead.

Another voice that we are quite good at allowing leeway for is expressed through the two words that pop out of our mouth too quickly, "What if?"

"What if" is like putting on the emergency break, bringing us to a sudden stop in fear, or perhaps rolling to a stop as the fear and "what if" questions build and take over. "What if" can stop us, paralyze us. It creates excuses posing as relief at remaining in the status quo, if not going backwards or to our safe hiding place. Most of the time the "what if" never materializes, and if it does, we have the power to say, "so what?!" and keep going, not letting it get in the way. Perhaps "what if" can even teach us what we need to know so that we can move to something better. You get the drift. I am quite confident that every reader has been or is challenged by those two pesky little words with the question mark.

If you feel creative, design a ceremony or a ritual for when you need to release the gremlins and saboteurs into the ether, far, far away from having an undesired effect on your dreams. Claim your power without apology!

Old stories, beliefs and imprints that do not serve

This is a deeper dive than saboteurs and gremlins, though they are close relatives. The saboteurs and gremlins love to latch on to the old stories, beliefs, and imprints as part of their nourishment.

Each of us has our own. Let me share one of the biggest imprints on me that I continue to deconstruct, followed by stepping into the story I want to create and believe instead. I will discipline myself to keep it short because it has had its way of running wild with me and keeping me limited. I will bullet this and I know you will understand . . . and if it is not one of your imprints that needs revision, by all means insert your own.

- My money story:

- We can't afford it

- It's too expensive

- We can buy fabric and make a dress just like that for much less

- The phone bill will be too high . . . we need to write letters instead

- Taking many rides around roads and areas of beautiful homes as if they were for others and not for us, as much as I loved, loved, loved my home and property . . . there was still an unintended message

- Being very clear about those in the city who "have money" (i.e. not us)

- Eating out is too expensive and an extravagance

That's enough to get the gist. The funny or ironic thing is that hearing some of these statements so many times created more of an imprint than the reality of all the abundance we actually had and the happiness and joy of our own property. It didn't really matter that we did not belong to the country club but there was something in noting others as "members of the _____ Club" that felt like "us and them." A thread of lack felt stronger than the thread of plenty, and so the thread of lack became the story of my life . . . lack, fear of lack, assumption of lack, "not for me," and so much more.

It also tied in with our religious faith, which was based on being of service to others first. If I fast forward through these many layers to creating my own business, the tug of war became, "How can I possibly charge that?! I am not worth it," or "People will not be able to afford me" or "I should make myself affordable to all," even when it is documented that the less people pay, the less attention they pay to doing the work.

I have written dozens of pages and read at least that number of books (and still do) as to how to get over my decades-long money blocks, freeing myself to create a new story, one of abundance and not guilt, where I value my work by charging for my experience, leadership, wisdom, and expertise. Lest it seem like it is, this is not about getting rich. It is about letting go of the mindset, stories, and saboteurs that do not serve me.

We carry imprints about physical qualities, abilities, academic achievements, professions, dress, and likely hundreds more things that deplete us, limit us, and keep us in the small boxes rather than living fully who we know we are when we go to the depths, when we dive below the surface and truly KNOW. We do not need to let any of the old stories, imprints and beliefs hang on—and in freeing ourselves from what might be their generational lineage, we might also liberate our children and their children from these limiting beliefs, as well.

As I write this book and speak about it, I am in my late 60s. I am still out there with the metaphorical scythe and the shovel, cutting down and unearthing what holds me back that came from the stories handed down that I can clear.

Clear . . . clear . . . clear . . . and create the story you want to live. There is plenty of available support for you, if needed, so that you can do the work.

Creating benchmarks, action steps, and your own measuring device

While I am writing about designing the "third-third of life" in small, specific sections, it is usually the case that they are happening simultaneously, mixing together. It makes me imagine the ingredients of a delicious, delectable, mouth-watering dessert combined for a spectacular outcome, where everyone who tastes it asks if they can have the recipe.

Goals and actions steps are among the ingredients. It is so easy, especially if we have worked hard to reach this time of life, to hope that what we want will be hand delivered, even special delivery, to us. And yet, we are a species that must take action, and taking action most often has the best results when tied to goals and intentions. How you measure these may be more or less important to you. I know people who must have the spreadsheet or chart or hard evidence as a measure and they cannot move forward without benchmarks to be met along the way. Others seem to have as much success by creating solid goals, knowing that when they take the actions to match the goal they are, in effect, meeting their benchmarks. You need to do it the way that works best for you.

Goals, however, speed us along even if gifted in intuition, imagination, and entrepreneurialism. That little left-brain handle of knowing where we want to head can then open the door to the right-brain way of getting there.

Once I knew I wanted to become a coach, I created my goals for how to make it happen. These included financing, a timeline for completing the courses and certification, and mapping out the path with intention along with action steps to achieve becoming a Certified Professional Coactive Coach. Within the process, I was more than able to lean on my intuition and imagination and then lean into my entrepreneurial spirit and desires to create my business . . . hand in hand with having business goals and an action plan. Those continue to evolve as my business continues to evolve. Goals . . . action steps . . . measure . . . repeat—all surrounded and supported by the beauty of the way my brain works to makes the goals come to life and flourish.

It may be that all you need are two or three goals and two or three action steps per goal. This does not have to be a massive list or even an exhaustive one; however, similar to values, the goals and actions lead the way and are inextricable from your values as well . . . yes, for sure. It's a beautifully choreographed dance.

Designing How to Honor the Full Circle of Life

I have chosen to create a separate chapter for this. Knowing how this topic touches people in so many different ways, I wanted this first chapter to be about the life you are living. Thus, a deeper consideration of your final days or years and passing has its own space. I want to respect that you choose the right time for the reading, and I also want to encourage that you do not avoid it or return to the phrase "there's always tomorrow." Peace to you for the consideration of that natural aspect of the life circle.

Reflection

Perhaps you have designed and redesigned your life two or three times. Or it may be that this is the first time EVER you have given yourself the gift of doing so, finally making the choice that the "third-third" is what you want it to be, stepping into your knowing yourself and out of any "shoulds" so that dreams become a reality, no matter how small, big, or in between. Just like Goldilocks, you get to test the beds and the chairs and the porridge . . . too small, too big, just right . . . too hard, too soft, just right . . . too salty, too hot, just right. This process is about the "just right" for you right now . . . not what came before or what will be ten years from now. It is about JUST RIGHT, RIGHT NOW.

Taking time for reflection through this journey is invaluable. Pause. Listen to yourself and really *hear*. Write. Find someone with whom you can share your questions and thoughts and who will be happy to sift with you. Just like the old-fashioned sifters for baking, picture what gets through the tiny screen and what doesn't, what stays and what goes. It might be that walking meditation and being out in nature provide you with an environment in which to relax, mull things over, and notice what enlightening insights come to awareness. It is always great to step out of our work and construction spaces to a geography that is different and allows new perspectives. On occasion, when I do a walking meditation, I see a piece of nature that in some uncanny way informs my dream and my work. It surprises me, delights me, often brings an "aha!" moment and turns out to be a great gift.

The gift of time alone that you give yourself is also invaluable. There is no rush. There is being, being in, and being with. Letting it be. Letting yourself be.

Find a form of reflection that works best for you. Let yourself sink into it. Allow it to wash over you. Or perhaps create new vibrant energy. It is yours, all yours. It will lead you along the path of your design as a companion you cannot do without. I am quite sure there will be a grateful heart for its companionship and effect.

Celebrate your magnificent life

Perhaps you have gone from "I don't know!" to "OMG . . . have I actually created this life??!!" Or perhaps it has been one smooth transition from what was to what is now. It doesn't matter how you got here or how long it took. You are here now. You may feel like you have scaled an impossible mountain or flown down a ski trail you predicted you would never in a million years attempt. You may feel like you are finally floating, breathing, letting go of all the stuff you were holding on to, and now you are free—utterly free.

Whatever it feels like, it belongs to you. There is no time like the present to stop, acknowledge what you have done and where you are, and to dance in celebration of a beautiful dream coming to reality. Host a party and let everyone know just who you are and what you'll be up to from now on. Live it up if that's your style (or even if it's not, perhaps try it on!), light some candles, have a glass of your favorite beverage with a delicious dinner and let it all settle in, or sit in the most comfortable spot under the night sky.

CELEBRATE . . . CELEBRATE . . .
CELEBRATE . . . CELEBRATE . . .
CELEBRATE!

This is the first step of celebration . . . of your design and voice. More steps of celebration to come!

HONORING THE FULL CIRCLE OF LIFE

"We shall find peace. We shall hear angels. We shall see the sky sparkling with diamonds."

Anton Chekov

THINKING ABOUT MY OWN LIFE and my ongoing conversations with my daughter and other family members, I do recognize that my older adult years will eventually come to closure in my passing. Speaking about this is a natural completion to the design process; however, of all the aspects of these years to talk about, this one is, for most, the easiest and most tempting to avoid.

If avoidance is the choice it will be a huge loss of not addressing ultimately the most important topic. I consider this as I am smack dab in the middle of designing and living what I anticipate will be some of the richest experiences, friendships, and times of my whole life. I want my daughter and others to be able to hear about and honor what I want these years in good health to be for me. At the same time, I want to fully step into my own recognition of the ending/transition that will come, even as I hope to naturally age into passing from this physical presence. *Naturally age into* is a great phrase to describe what we all hope for. In the process of natural aging, especially the older one lives to be, there may develop mental, emotional, or physical limitations that create new circumstances.

It is in my heart to speak equally to my older years of life as I live it now and to my passing and what might occur on the final path. For some, it is easy to talk about the whole enchilada, as the saying goes. For others, it is easy to speak to life when it is brimming with energy, activities and independence, and much harder to face speaking about limitations and death/physical passing/transition. It is my goal and hope to ease the latter for you.

I hold admiration for cultures that seem to honor the cycle of birth, life, and death with less hesitation, fear, and angst, and openly speak about it rather than shy away from it. The complete cycle is one that is natural and one that we know will occur. Being with and accompanying elders to the end of their journey is as sacred as welcoming the new life of a baby. Perhaps for the moment, you can free yourself from whatever keeps you in avoidance and instead, be one with the nature of life . . . of all things that we know . . . flowers, trees, animals, and us. We all live the continuum of being born, of blooming, of all the beauty and life that come forth from our existence, to life ebbing away. To everything there is a season. Each of our lives is a season.

It is so interesting how we all know this as fact. We all recognize that there can be no birth without death, and yet we have created a cultural mindset in which death is difficult to discuss or is not discussed. Just as I do not want to see the end of the gorgeous bouquet my daughter gave me for Mother's Day, how much more challenging it can be to face watching the end of life approach and the bouquet of experiences and connections beginning to wither. Soon, these blooms will be but memories.

But the flowers in the vase do not all drop off at one time and into one heap. Rather, it is a process, even when seemingly sudden, and so it is with our lives. It was such with my father. One Saturday morning in November of 1999 I received a phone call from my sister that started with her saying it was a call I did not want to get. During the night, our father had suffered a heart attack in his sleep and did not wake up. Some might say it was like the whole flower dropping off at once, but I see a different perspective. He was 91. Three times the day before, he filled the trailer on the back of his car with wood from trees on our property that had been felled by a hurricane. He took the wood to a church friend who was recuperating from surgery. My dad was still driving. He had sawed up 11 trees by himself and stacked the wood. He was blooming even as his body inside was beginning the journey of ending. Petals were falling even as they could not be seen, his physical body wearing down even as he chose to keep being and doing all that he loved. It was exactly the way of departing this life that he would have chosen. A notice in the church bulletin the next morning said, "A mighty oak has fallen." What a beautiful way of phrasing my dad's passing in that he had been working with the trees that day and taking joy in sharing their bounty with a friend in need.

I believe the oak was bending even when we could not see its gradual movement. So yes, both/and, sudden, and yet the organs slowing down so that they could no longer endure that kind of work. I missed, and still miss, the opportunity to say goodbye to him and yet there are no regrets at all. There was nothing unsaid. We all knew that he was not going to be one to sit around and wait for death to come to him, even as he was not necessarily inviting it to visit that day. For him and everything I knew about him, that was the natural ending. He naturally aged into taking leave from his body.

With my mother, it was much more of a gradual aging process, with a marked shift from being able to take care of herself independently to needing daytime companions while my sister was at work and finally, to 24-hour hospice care. We were extremely fortunate that both parents were able to live at home until their passing, though my mother's journey to that time was slower and a more visible seeing of a "petal at a time" dropping off. She met her goal of living to 100, and very soon after that mark in time it was time for her to say goodbye. I was privileged to be there in those moments. I knew when I arrived to be with her on what turned out to be her last day that the scent of death was in her room, its arrival making itself known in her body. It was time. I will never forget how, when I arrived, she grasped my necklace as I leaned over to kiss her hello and held on for an extra moment. I see her face each time I put on the necklace.

For each family and for each one of us, death/transition/passing will show up differently. In the knowing of that, perhaps we can prepare ourselves better for its arrival, though at times even the idea of preparation seems impossible.

The unknown as well as what are often unexpected, shocking circumstances are part of my "why" for writing this book and speaking as often as I can so that families know all is in place well ahead of time. I want to fully acknowledge that while we hope for the grace of the natural and complete aging cycle, there are times when sudden illness or accidents claim lives, which is all the more reason to create the opportunity to do this work as soon as we can or will allow ourselves.

HONORING THE FULL CIRCLE OF LIFE

There is a beautiful poem by Mary Oliver, "When Death Comes."

When death comes
like the hungry bear in autumn;
when death comes and takes all the bright coins from his
purse
to buy me, and snaps the purse shut;
when death comes
like the measle-pox
when death comes
like an iceberg between the shoulder blades,
I want to step through the door full of curiosity, wondering:
what is it going to be like, that cottage of darkness?

And therefore I look upon everything
as a brotherhood and a sisterhood,
and I look upon time as no more than an idea,
and I consider eternity as another possibility,
and I think of each life as a flower, as common
as a field daisy, and as singular,
and each name a comfortable music in the mouth,

tending, as all music does, toward silence,
and each body a lion of courage, and something
precious to the earth.

When it's over, I want to say all my life
I was a bride married to amazement.
I was the bridegroom, taking the world into my arms.

When it's over, I don't want to wonder
if I have made of my life something particular, and real.

I don't want to find myself sighing and frightened,
or full of argument.

I don't want to end up simply having visited this world.

This book is all about living fully and, in the end, not simply having visited this world. As part of not having simply visited this world, I invite you to embrace the reality of the whole with no hesitation, with no fears of conversation, and with joy that the circle of life can be honored and celebrated fully. In that mindset and intention, I also invite you to openly and with grace embrace conversation and communication about how to be ready, so that when the time comes there is the full capacity to honor the life of the one who passes rather than being mired in the details and missed opportunities. Rest assured, knowing that critical documents and information have been shared and made known, including any ways in which you want to be part of creating the gathering that takes place after passing. As part of living fully, allow for preparations to be complete and clearly communicated.

Of one thing I am absolutely certain. Even if the conversation calls on all the strength you have to enter into it, the results will be gratitude, relief, and freedom—for you *and* your loved ones. You will know that all is in good order and that these years can be spent in fullness of living, and this is a gift beyond measure. Step into it with confidence, knowing that it will be this.

Let us allow for the beauty of passing to be honored in its fullness, overflowing with grace and wonder, compassion, acknowledgement, magnificence, and love.

If and when tears flow, anywhere and at any time in the reading of this book, allow them. They, too, are a natural part of living the wholeness of life.

PART II

Chronos time
By the clock
Most often
All of our busyness
Deadlines
Planning
Rushing
No time
Too busy
On overload
"Gotta go"
Not stopping
Even if living

A fulfilling life

Kairos time
Time of the soul
Relationship
Connection
Presence
No clock
Being

Part II
Is
About
Kairos time

IMAGINING THE LIFE-GIVING CONVERSATION
(OR PERHAPS REIMAGINING)

"Look past your thoughts
so you can drink the pure
nectar of this moment."

Rumi

YOU ENTER THIS PART OF the book with your brilliantly designed life guiding you, even if still in process. The design has and continues to come to life, for it will take on beautiful facets and reveal mysteries and moments you cannot possibly yet know. You are standing fast, grounded, and centered in the fulfillment life brings you; you rejoice that you made the conscious decision to "play full out," to be fully you, and to live the life you want to live in this "third-third." It does not mean that there are no interruptions or intrusions; however, as an outcome of living in your choice, you will face them with more strength and resiliency.

It is important to remember the above paragraph, for here we begin to wade into the waters of how to step into life-giving conversations with family to share the design with them. Here we begin to step up the steps. If designing your life was your first 10,000, now we start the climb with 10,001. While we welcome the mysteries of life that reveal themselves in the designs we create and surprise us as if opening an unexpected gift, it is a choice to share those decisions with family members. Sharing assures that they do not meet a dark, challenging mystery when the time comes that they are responsible for managing your care plan or your estate. You may recall that in the very beginning of the book one of the WHYs of this writing is to encourage you to let your wishes and plans be known before you are unable to articulate them.

It is now time to initiate the intentional plan for how to step into having an essential conversation, a life-giving conversation. I want to begin with a brief story.

It is one thing for me to write this book. It is another for me to practice it. That is the truth. It's rather like coaching my clients. Often, when reflecting on a coaching session, I realize I have also coached myself. It is not unusual for me to stop to ask if I take to heart and practice that which I am skilled at helping others take to heart and practice.

During the writing and editing of this book I made a significant geographical move (a major priority of my own third-third design) and have gone on several small trips. Before leaving for one of the short trips and when this writing was particularly fresh in my mind, I realized that if anything happened to me, I had given my daughter some of the important information, but not all. "So, author of the book, get busy and do what you are writing about with such dedication!"

With that nudge, I created a list of my most important passwords and tucked them in a place with other important documents. That was easy. I then stopped to compose a last minute email to my daughter before getting in my car to tell her where I was leaving the information, skirting my own intention of having as much as possible be face to face. As I began to type I found myself with extremely mixed emotions and even a sense of fear and physical shakiness. It was so clear that even with all of my conviction about this topic, I did not want to talk about the "what if." I also did not want the message to start the crazy effect of presuming that since I was giving her information that something might happen to me. I found so much getting stirred up. It took me totally by surprise. That one small task brought me into stark realization and clarity about how easily procrastination can happen. It also reinforced once again just how crucial this communication is.

There are as many ways of being a family as there are families in the world. Even with hundreds of books written about the possibilities for how families can come together, and an equal number written on dysfunction of families, there is no one size fits all. I maintain that in most families, there is both the spectacular coming together coupled with or complemented by dysfunction—because that is life. I do not believe there is any such thing as perfect.

That is just as true of this book. It is not a perfect book with perfect information, which is why I am writing it as more of a guide containing musings, possibilities, and suggestions that I hope will be helpful. Ultimately, you are the one to choose how and when to communicate with your family. What I will be relentless about is the message that NOW IS THE TIME . . . before "too late" comes, so that your family does not live in preventable regrets and stress (barring unforeseen life changing situations).

So you say, "If you want to talk about stress . . . just let me tell you about my family and how much stress there is in having this conversation with them." I imagine it so clearly. And yes, perhaps there will be. It will still be less stress than letting the conversation go. This is for those of you who shy away from the threshold you have to step over to saying, "Yes, I'll do this."

Imagine sitting with your family. Perhaps you imagine that you are sitting across from them or in a circle. You look at each one and see the individual members in your mind's eye. Some families seem to have all sweetness and light, with nary a disagreement or varied ways of thinking (though often buried underneath that are unspoken thoughts so as to not ripple the waters). They always seem on board together. If that is your family, you might want to skip this step because you will likely dive right into the conversation and have no worry at all about sharing your thoughts.

Most, however, humorously ask the question at times of how the members of the family ever ended up being born into it! My sister and I have said that to each other many times over the years . . . joking that the other one was the wrong baby sent home from the nursery.

As you imagine your family sitting with you right now, what is your mindset? Is it the mindset you want to stay in as you prepare to talk with them? Is it a mindset that is positive or that depletes you? Is it of joy and confidence or fear and "less than?" Of trust or doubt? Of being grounded and certain about who you are and what you want or of shakiness and scattered uncertainties that only crop up as you think about the conversation? How many times when we are alone we stand in total confidence and assuredness about our choices and decisions. Yet, when we get in front of others, we melt into puddles of nerves and worry about what will be said or the questions that will be asked or the critiques we will face. It's rather hilarious, actually, that others can so easily shift us out of who we know ourselves to be and what we want into wondering if we are living up to their expectations—even once we've grown to be the older, wiser, respected and revered adults in the family. It is hard to get over the wanting to please mindset—and I encourage you in this sentence, right now, to let it go. This is about your life fulfilling you. Yes, *you*.

You get to model exactly how you want to be seen and heard; in many ways older adults are, in these moments, mentors, models and way-showers for other family members, whether children or your own siblings and peers. You might be the first one to set the bar high. It is an opportunity to create a new communication model that I hope will eventually eradicate any need for this book. You get to choose how to be present . . . whether you even think of it consciously or not, you are always choosing how to be present to others.

As you look at your family in this moment of imagination, what are the stories you have made up about how each one, and how they as a whole, will respond to you as you talk about your "third-third of life?" What are assumptions you are holding? These may include stereotypes and stories that come to mind, including from your own childhood family system. Jot them down and read them out loud. Are they inspiring and life-giving, or do they bring up the fears, hesitations, and nervousness about moving forward? What is underneath what you are imagining? What is the history? We all have in our lineage—the good, the bad, and the ugly, so to speak. It is not about glossing over that. We can access the grace and thoughtfulness to change what is created now. It is so powerful to keep that "knowing" at the forefront because it can be easily dismissed.

"Oh, my family will never change. They think anyone over 60 is heading into a downhill spiral. When they get to this place they will see that it is not so and yet I am tired of feeling like I have to prove myself."

"You have no idea what you are proposing . . . it will never work in this group . . . are you kidding me?"

IMAGINING THE LIFE-GIVING
CONVERSATION

"If you only knew my children and how they worry about me at this stage of life, in love of course, you would know that every piece of what I say will be gone over with their version of the fine-toothed comb . . . very, very fine-toothed."

"My children want so much for me to live my own life so they can live theirs; however, they can't help themselves by double-checking everything. I love that about them and it also makes me crazy, so I see this as a hundred conversations. We'll be talking (and likely negotiating) for years."

"I know one of my children will support me 100% and that the other two will think I have gone off the deep end. They will all appreciate knowing where to locate the legal documents and keys and such, but in terms of my choosing to continue living independently until I can't . . . well . . . that will be another perspective for those two."

The above are actual statements from Baby Boomer + friends I spoke with while writing this book. While some know exactly how to navigate these conversations, many are still searching.

How does exploring these stories and assumptions impact you, personally, in a way that will influence your capacity to speak about your life? What do they bring up for you and what is it that you might feel called to reflect on and come to peace with on your own as you anticipate bringing others into the circle of your plans and wishes?

If you are struggling in any way and being pulled out of strength, take time to honor the feelings running through you. Thank the challenging ones for having their place, for often they crop up to try to protect us in their own strange way. Then give yourself permission to completely reimagine what is possible, what you desire, what is energizing and positive—and usher the challenging feelings out.

Audaciously begin to replace the old, stereotypical, past history "voices" with a new mindset that will create the fresh story and experience that you want to leave as that model I mention above.

Take time, silly and even vulnerable as it might seem to some of you, and perhaps a very new experience, to write positive, affirming statements about the beauty of family communication that will be not only life-giving but also life-affirming. Think individually of a family member (or person with whom you will be talking) and write about that person. You might also want to write statements about you that you shy away from doing. These do not have to be novels . . . they can be bullets. What you will find as you take time to do this is that you will begin to think of how each person might respond when you are together, and this will bring you in to the full perspective of the family dynamic. While it is easy to say, "Oh, I already know what that is, don't you worry," it is quite different to stop to give each individual time and space with you in your mind and heart.

Imagine yourself accessing your courage and being present with and to family members, creating this as a time of celebration of life. Know that you can look each one in the eye expecting them to respond out of their kindest, most compassionate, loving heart spaces. Imagine that this has all the beautiful possibility of being a transformative time with family, perhaps even a healing time. It will be so individual.

In the imagining and reimagining you can beautifully come to this:

"Having worked through these assumptions and stories, letting some go and in process of letting more challenging ones go, I cannot wait for the opportunity to sit with my family and share my plans. It is exciting to feel this level of confidence and how happy I am in my certainty of what I want." This is an example of a spectacular affirmation!

My hope and belief for you is that at the end of this step, you'll be willing and able to imagine a life-giving conversation with your unique stamp, one in which you will be affirmed, honored, respected, and thanked for having done such exceptional preparation and for the giving of this gift.

Should you choose to jot down thoughts about each family member, the following examples may prove helpful:

_____ – Appreciates clear, concise communication that is not drawn out; will likely spend less rather than more time around feelings. I will try to honor that and somehow acknowledge it even though I know I will need to expand a bit for _____.

_____ – May begin to get teary even as we start to talk together; thoughts about death are especially difficult due to an early trauma of having lost a best friend. I want to take a few minutes to remember his friend and yet be in recognition that this is a different conversation, one that will ultimately help prepare him.

_____ – Would rather talk about anything than this! I want to find a way to preface why this is so important and to ask for patience and understanding. In fact, I want to reflect on how I can bring a bit of humor or celebration into the relationship, not overdoing, but to try to lighten it a bit.

If some reframing and new perspectives are needed, you might create your own intention. This is a very individual choice for you, as are the words you use, but here is an example you may use as a springboard

"I choose to believe that while acknowledging any awkwardness, discomfort, and possible disinterest, we will create a space of understanding, even if only a beginning to be continued at another time close to this one (as in, I will not put this off!). Most of all, I want my love and respect for my children to be as clear and obvious as any communication about plans for my transition. I trust them to join me in ways that may not seem obvious right now but that I am going to hold for all of us."

I have no doubt that some of you are considering speaking with each child individually and I hear that even if I cannot see you. I really do. Let me suggest, however, two things.

One relates to the age-old game of "telephone." Each person will no doubt hear your words subjectively as much as objectively, which leaves the conversation open to interpretation. That, in turn, may unintentionally create misheard or misunderstood or misinterpretation. That, in turn, may unintentionally create a domino effect of disagreeing with what was said even if you said the exact same words to each one. You know where I am going with this. It is not that that can't also happen if you meet together, but the chances are minimized.

Second, one of my hopes is that while a conversation or multiple conversations over time might feel like the biggest challenge you have yet encountered (though I hope not), it is also a time to create a new or additional way of being in touch as a family and even a "bringing together" on your behalf. I am extremely hesitant to use the word healing, and yet I believe that these moments have the capacity to diminish long held differences.

As you can tell through the pages of this book, I trust you to make the best choice for you.

ALIGNING YOUR VALUES WITH YOUR COMMUNICATION

"Praise the bridge that
carried you over."

George Colman the Younger

A LIGNING VALUES WITH COMMUNI-cation is like crossing a bridge and taking that which is most important with you as you shift from your thoughts and decisions—an internal process—into the conversation with others—an external one. It is holding and carrying the continuity of what is most important to you into this space of sharing words.

I used to think of alignment with a rather limited mindset and realize that there was nothing at all wrong but that I was not seeing all the possibilities for how alignment can show up. Let me see if I can articulate my ever-expanding sense of possibility without losing the point of this section.

Alignment has numerous meanings and representations. It does not necessarily mean static or always in a straight line. For the sake of this book, I refer to alignment as matching up, being in sync, working seamlessly together, and not tripping or crashing because of misalignment.

When things are aligned they support, guide, and assist us in staying the course. If we find ourselves out of alignment it is, perhaps, time to let go of a part of life or material possession that needs to be let go of, that no longer sustains us. It may well be time for a personal life tune-up.

Here are some simple examples: when you walk out the front door of your home you want to be lined up directly with the front steps or walk and if there are steps, those having been built evenly spaced is optimal.

When the tires of a car are out of alignment, the car feels wobbly and the steering wheel vibrates. If the alignment issue is not taken care of it can eventually lead to an accident. When we feel the shimmy, we know it is time to get the car in for repair. We also feel uncomfortable and nervous driving it.

Our bodies function optimally when their parts are in alignment . . . teeth, spine, knees, hips, etc. Misalignment, if not attended to, can result in being off balance, in pain, slower than we like, and perhaps living in a debilitated state.

Binoculars, if dropped, can get out of alignment so that what you see through one lens is off kilter with what is seen through the other lens. When my glasses tilt one way or another as I am typing, it is the same.

I remember reading *House* by Tracy Kidder many years ago and the ways in which the architect, builder, and owner need to alter plans so that the design of all aspects of the house will be in alignment. Often it is the builder who discovers that what appeared so imaginative and delightfully unique in the design will simply not work in the actual building. She knows she is responsible for the structure being sound. As I write this book I am observing new condos being built on the next lot, and I watch how frequently the construction workers measure and use the level and look and eye and debate so as to be impeccable in the alignment and smooth function of every part.

My ongoing mulling about alignment has brought a couple of random examples to mind. I think of the ingredients of a recipe being in alignment. Not all ingredients are of the same proportions or taste but when combined, create s delicious, mouthwatering nibble.

Or what might appear to be random placement of art, so far away from a straight-line display, might create perfect alignment of the whole. It might even appear messy at first but when one stands back and is open to a different perspective about how something should be displayed, it is obvious that it works.

When we open up and let go of assumptions about what alignment should look like, which I dare say are often very black and white, it is amazing and beautiful to see the possibilities.

Alignment with our values is a guiding beacon, a lighthouse, if you will, for these conversations. It is also possible that the light has to shine in and on some messiness, just as an auto repair shop often takes things apart to put them back in alignment. That is perfectly ok. Alignment in relationship is not about perfection, as it might need to be with a car or house. It is, however, like a spark plug that connects us to what we most deeply long for and keeps us centered.

There are so many ways in which people work to stay in alignment or may be called back into alignment, whether on their own or as part of a group. In a profession, it is making sure that outcomes of a project or role are in alignment with the mission and vision of a business, or that a speaking engagement is in alignment with the overall theme of a conference. It may be that we begin to feel wear and tear emotionally in such a way that we can tell we are out of alignment with what we want in life . . . we have an "off course" feeling. Being out of alignment can cause physical, emotional, and mental distress, or might mean it would be in our best interest to choose a different profession.

You get the gist. We are called forth to repairs, pain relief, getting back on track, or feeling whole and functioning well again, which may mean making new choices in our lives. And yes, it can be a bit disorienting and messy in the process.

Sometimes it is not so drastic. We can stay in alignment with quick touch points and check-ins with ourselves and we can engage in preventative maintenance so as to quickly bring the wobble back to steady, just like the oil change every 2,500 miles. The more we check in over time, the fewer the surprises and the less likely we are to be caught off guard.

Look back at your values, remembering that values can be religious, moral, or ethical but do not necessarily need to be any of those. It is easy to list them in an initial exercise and then drift away from staying in sync with them, in resonance with them. As you know, values are a center, an anchor, a support beam, part of a map that guides how we live. Yes, they can change according to life circumstances; most often, however, there are some that are fundamental and unchanging. If you did not get specific in Part I, I urge you to stop now and do so because of the importance of alignment with values to the conversation with family. Let me give you an example so that the difference is seen.

ALIGNING YOUR VALUES WITH YOUR COMMUNICATION

To go back to an earlier example in the book, if I say a value is "being a good person" it is a lovely goal to want to be that; however, what does "being a good person" look like in reality? When you dig more deeply into a general or even generic value, you uncover the layers, the specifics of what it truly means to you. I have had clients interpret being a good person as never saying what they think because they also want to keep the peace, whereas someone else says that being a good person means they are always willing to be honest and speak their truth so as to never cover up their thoughts and feelings. It is not about right or wrong. It is about being very specific and clear.

For the sake of this conversation, another reason it is so important right here, right now, is that everyone in your family might hold the same expressed value/word and yet it might mean something different to each person. Taking time on this is not to beat a dead horse . . . it is, rather, to discern clearly if the way in which you are going to hold the "third-third of life" conversation with your family is in alignment with your values or if it might need some realignment.

Another example. A value is honesty. Yet, when you come together on this big topic you know that being completely honest is going to set someone off. So you compromise and say, "Well, I am going to beat around the bush a bit on this . . . or . . . I am going to couch this in language that won't get _____ upset and then when the time comes, I'll be more honest." Then you catch yourself . . . out of alignment!

It is easy, understandably so, to begin sliding an inch or two down the slippery slope, usually in the name of not creating conflict and dis-ease. Think forward. Being clear and aligning with your values now will spare everyone much more pain and potential dissension later. It is far more worth it than you might feel or even know. It might even mean imagining children having a conversation ten years after you are gone saying something like, "I know at the time we really gave Mom (or Dad or Mom and Dad etc.) a hard time when she got us together to talk about her life and the end of her life, but wow . . . right now I wish she could know how incredibly grateful I am . . . we are . . . because she spared us the messiness of what so many of my friends are going through."

Yes . . . for real. It is far more apt to be that than staying frustrated. And if they stay frustrated, you'll never know anyway—but at least you'll know that you did the right thing. The wide-open possibility is that what might seem, feel, or initially give goose bumps or worse, wondering how in the world you will navigate some of the random and disheveled moments, can turn into just right alignment. Live in possibility. And trust.

Alignment check

- Review your values. You might even want to add a new one or two for this time and this gathering.

- Specifically, what are your values around family? Communication? And your soul's desire?

- What kind of conversation will allow you to, will call you forth to staying in alignment? What will that look and feel like?

- What intentions do you want to set for yourself to keep your values in the forefront, no matter what? I will go more deeply into intentions in the next step so if setting intentions is new to you and you wonder how to set them, stay tuned.

- Anticipate what might look off kilter or not quite as you imagined at first and stay in openness to the arrangements and the dialogue creating their own design that works for your family.

Know that if you or a conversation feels as if it is shifting out of alignment, you have the resources you need within you. Take a moment to pause, breathe, observe, listen, and ask yourself an excellent question to ask in such moments, silently, or perhaps even out loud (you'll know which): "What's needed now?" With insight, move back into realignment grounded in your presence . . . to self and to others . . . and trust your intuition to guide as your values shine the beacon of light.

DESIGNING INTENTIONAL TIME WITH FAMILY

"People are made of flesh
and blood and a moral
fibre called courage."

Mignon McLaughlin

FOR THE SAKE OF ILLUSTRATION, I will start this chapter with another story about Annie, the dog from downstairs that has her own bed in my apartment. I wanted my daughter and a friend to meet her so they could see this wonderful little creature I talk about all the time. Annie's owner opened the back door and Annie ran up the stairs, undoubtedly anticipating that I would be the only one she would see. Running into the kitchen and finding two others there, she came to a halt, and, I noticed a bit later, had even peed a little on the floor in her startled state. I assumed she would be just as happy and friendly with my daughter and friend as with me and yet she went totally silent and wanted to escape back downstairs, not welcoming their gestures to pet her and make friends. It was clear that she was not at ease with unexpected new people. It took a while and a bit of coaxing for me to get her to come back up once I was alone again.

My surface intention was for Annie to love being greeted by others and they by her. It was also based in an assumption that of course she would thrive on meeting more people. I was wrong. I had not even stopped to consider what it might be like for Annie.

If I had taken time to be intentional in my design for the meeting, I would have asked her owner if Annie enjoys meeting new people or if there was a way better than others to introduce them. Intentional design can save us from assumptions backfiring. So often what we reflect back on with the term "it was all in good intentions" also means it was all with certain assumptions. Both can be true.

There are the random intentions that we actually don't even think about in the moment, which are unspoken, and then there is intentional design. This is my very personal view of how the two differ.

So often we say something to the effect of, "Well, I know she had the best intentions." I spoke that about my mother earlier in the book and it is absolutely true. At the same time, in the moment of an action or words spoken, a person is not necessarily being intentional about them or in a conscious decision, e.g. "Right now I am going to choose to say this or do this."

It more likely happens out of an unspoken, understood intentional place and we usually try to give others the benefit of the doubt even when the impact is difficult. A child might act spontaneously to help clear the table and drop and break a dish. The child's intention was a lovely one and perhaps the dish was simply too big or slippery. The child did not stand by the table and say, "It is with intentional design that I am going to help clear the table." It was likely a spontaneous idea with the unspoken intention of helping.

Let's look at how to design intentions and design **with** intention.

As I mentioned earlier, most mornings I design my day with written intentions. They are not commitments but intentions, my best hopes and goals for the day. One of my intentions for today was to sit for most of the afternoon and write this step. I want to write. I love getting into the flow. It will make me happy if at the end of the day I feel I have accomplished this. At the same time, there are multiple things pulling me away: It's a holiday, I'm antsy to get out of my house and go exploring my new geography, I don't feel like settling into anything, I just want to putter, etc. And yet, when I look at the card on which I have written my intentions for today, I am pulled back to what I truly want. I am deliberate in my intentions. They are not "shoulds" because the word "should" has basically exited my vocabulary. I will speak to that a little later in this step.

Another intention for today was to finish hanging things on the walls of my new home rather than continuing to see the two or three things that are left to hang leaning up against the walls. Check! It might be that that intention allowed me to putter before settling in to writing and yet I accomplished it and am much happier as I walk around. In its own way, it helped me step into the writing intention. These intentions were not mutually exclusive.

Designing with intention pairs fabulously with mindset. It is also a choice. I find that when I set strong intentions, I create, by extension, a positive frame of mind. Intentions are like first cousins of goals. They can be short-term (for today), or longer (for five years), or ongoing. Sometimes I carry over an intention from one day to the next even if I have kept it the day before, especially when it comes to writing or working on other longer-term projects. It is a declaration. It is purposeful. It has an outcome envisioned. It can be easy or it can be downright bold and courageous or call me into my heart space. It is "in the spirit of . . ." and is something I consistently will to happen and then act on.

Why is this step so important? It is because choosing how to live our life and how to share that choice (or choices) with our family is not an "oh, by the way . . ." as we are saying goodbye or over a cup of tea or when everyone is feeling rushed or not feeling well. When those kinds of conversations take place, it is often the case that people are not really listening carefully, that we might not be speaking carefully, and afterwards a common thought is, "Oh, I wish I had remembered to say _____ _____ _ ____." This conversation with our family members is not helter-skelter time.

Here are some ideas. Please feel free to add, delete, create your own from scratch to fit you and your family, and know that there can be a design for multiple conversations, not just one. It's a big deal, so take your time! At the end of an initial conversation that comes from your designed intentions, you might think of a new one to add.

- Dare to dream! Think of this as a huge blank canvas, similar to when you created your own "third-third of life" blueprint. Allow it to be magical, colorful, animated, real, dynamic, authentic, truth telling without apology or compromise, and filled with joy and the knowing that you are giving a gorgeously wrapped gift. Stop for a moment to really picture this. Maybe you even bring party favors . . . what a great idea!

- Combining your thoughts from Imagining (Reimagining) and Aligning (Realigning), how do you want to create a new approach to what is often labeled a "difficult conversation that no one wants to have?"

- In a refreshing new mindset, begin to design the conversation. It will take time and care. Allow yourself time to play with it by stepping out of the rule that this must be a completely dead serious gathering (no pun intended). Allow humor to join you if that fits you. How do you want to include affirming moments, humorous moments, open listening moments, quiet, reflective moments of some space, and other types of moments that suit your family dynamic?

- Take some time to think about each person who is going to be present. What do you know about each one and the dynamic of the whole that calls for thoughtful consideration about wording, tone, and in an intention of keeping the family in a space of peace and care for one another? How can you make room for each personality to be heard, yet not allow for potential to move you out of your confidence? If there are extended family members it is good to set an intention about who this gathering is for. Only your children to begin with, or children and spouses or partners? I would kindly suggest that it is not a conversation of which young children need to be a part. It is also going to be a different kind of conversation if your immediate family does not include children but may be siblings or other relatives. It may be that your "family" is made up of a cluster of dear friends. Families come in all different configurations.

- Where might you have the conversation that will encourage and allow everyone to feel comfortable? Your home? Someone else's home? A beautiful inn? On a gorgeous hike to a place that is special to you? Over a favorite meal? Around a beach campfire? What feels like a fabulous neutral setting? What I would suggest is that it is not a conversation begun after everyone has had very much alcohol, though over a glass of wine might be fine. After two or three glasses, not so much.

You are the master designer, even if you have never considered yourself one before. Now is the time and yes, NOW IS THE TIME. Allow yourself time and space to design and reflect and redesign . . . with the caveat that you do not give yourself permission to use that as an excuse or to put off the conversation. Perhaps share your thoughts with a close friend as practice, someone who will keep the information confidential. Only you know if that would be wise or not. Or practice with just you, saying out loud some of what you want to communicate, especially if you know this is stepping into territory that feels risky and vulnerable.

It will be fully worth it.

CELEBRATE

"I can no other
answer make but
thanks, and thanks."

William Shakespeare

WHY? WHY A STEP OF celebration? Isn't it enough to have gotten this far? Do I have to drag this out more? Stay with me here and please know that this is in your timeline. It might be that you have one conversation or that conversations may take place over time.

As I look back to my family's conversation by the barn on that beautiful summer day, sitting in our circle of chairs, I am quite sure there was a moment of acknowledgement that our parents sharing with us what they wanted at the end of their lives. I know each of us held a space that honored the gratefulness for the difference made through their talking with us. I am also quite sure that like the usual response after such conversations, we all got up and went back to whatever it was we were doing. It did not flow into a celebration. And truth be told, I'd like a do-over. We were a family of minimal celebration so it could have been small and brief . . . but I find myself wishing we'd done something to mark the moment.

As with all other habits and traditions of families, celebrations are as varied as the number of families (except, perhaps, for the children's birthday party model . . . but that is a whole other book . . . or you can feel free to talk with me . . . ha!). They can be quiet, candlelit, understated, boisterous on the town dancing, pizza around an outdoor fire pit, and a million more designs. Some families live for celebrations while others are less inclined to that model. There is no right or wrong.

Whatever your way of celebrating, I do want to say without hesitation that when conversations this "big" happen, especially when in the context of transformative perspectives and presence after, perhaps, fearful anticipation and avoidance, there is a call for celebrating in some way. It will bring full circle what has been a true journey and intentional decision to make sure that all family members have been gifted with critically important information. These essential life-giving conversations may, in fact, become a catalyst for a new way of communicating with one another and may have a contagious or domino effect on extended family members.

I think of several components of celebration, which might lead to more than one kind of celebration. Wouldn't that be fun!

As you think back through the whole sequence of steps, there is the celebration of who you are and that you have made a conscious decision about how to live your life . . . *yours* to decide and yours to live. It is where you are now, not where you were twenty or thirty years ago. Life is thriving; there is no stagnating for this "third-third." You might even shock your family by what you choose to do, in which case, hurray for you! That is celebration number one.

It is a celebration of where children are in their lives and making their life one of breathing, of knowing, of being able to put aside wondering how in the world they are going to handle your getting older and what that might bring. You get to celebrate, and they get to celebrate, where they are now. It is also the knowledge that they have not yet traveled your path and that it might take some extra courage on their part to step into a resounding "Yes!" and awesome support for and of you.

It is celebrating persistence, clarity, commitment, and intention, honoring your full voice, dreams, confidence, joy, and perhaps even childlike giddiness.

It is a celebration of life itself. It is celebrating that when we are on this journey we can decide that old stories and family belief systems can be explored and rewritten. Assumptions can be put aside for what is real. There is no one way, and for all the books written about family, it is for each family to design who they want to be and how they want to live. This is a time to celebrate doing away with labels, whether it is terrible twos, the woes of adolescence, mid-life crisis or all the depleting stories we internalize about aging. It is saying yes to changing those and shifting, if not doing away with expectations.

It is a celebration of the exquisite flow of freedom for all . . . freedom for a child to be a child to the freedom of an older adult to be an older adult, all living life to the fullest as it circles from the moment of conception to the moment of passing over. So often, rather than flow with it, we make life (yes, *we* make it) be so much harder than necessary by reinforcing the expectations, rules, beliefs that are simply stories that have been subjectively created over time.

I have seen the transformation that happens when we let the "shoulds" and the old paradigms go and the fullness of each age is honored without labels and criticisms, when the gift of life is seen even through the lens of Alzheimer's or a limited ability. Again, this is not about life being perfect. Life is not. It is about life being genuine and realizing, for the sake of this particular book, that those in their senior years still see themselves as all the ages they have been before and do not need to be treated with kid gloves or as if they are fragile.

Just as we prepare for birth, for those very first months and years of life, we prepare for the later years and the same exquisite beauty and uniqueness of when the older adult was born. Because each one was, you know, and we so easily forget that. Once in a while, photos remind us, but too often we only think of each other as the age we are now, forgetting what came before. So often a beautiful quote by Madeleine L'Engle in her book *Walking on Water: Reflections on Faith and Art* pops into my head and heart: " . . . we must never forget any part of ourselves. As of this writing I am sixty-one years old in chronology. But I am not an isolated, chronological numerical statistic. I am sixty-one, and I am also four, and twelve, and fifteen, and twenty-three, and thirty-one and forty-five, and . . . and . . . and. If we lose any part of ourselves, we are thereby diminished. If I cannot be thirteen or sixty-one simultaneously, part of me has been taken away."

Take full permission to make this celebration special, even if it is the only time you have ever done so. Celebrate the whole of life. Take a vacation together and if that is asking way too much (!), dinner or a gathering that suits you all. It is a time to say thank you to one another now . . . NOW IS THE TIME . . . rather than waiting to express gratitude years later when the whole family is no longer together to hear it. It's great to keep the gratitude going and for this whole essential, life-giving conversation journey to be a model for all who come later, but not at the expense of treasuring the moments of gratitude now. Even if blushing and embarrassed, let thanks be shared with one another.

It is one part of life that can be lived fully, no matter what has come before. Live it and celebrate it in joy!

PART III

How often we wanted
To be grown up
When we were
Still children

Now

We enter years
When we want
To continue to
Be the children
And yet are called
To live out
Being the grown-ups
We have become

FOR CHILDREN OF
BABY BOOMERS +

"I realize now that no matter how old my parents are, they are still independent and deserve to live their lives freely and as joyfully as possible until and unless there is significant change. I want to support them even though it makes me nervous sometimes"

"It never occurred to me that I might be called on to be the one to initiate a conversation about honoring the cycle of life and how to make that a family conversation. I get we might all rather tiptoe around it forever and I also get that forever might mean too late."

"I love that I feel permission to raise this whole topic and do not have to wait. It will ultimately bring us all peace of mind."

Real conversations

YES, YOU, A BABY BOOMER +, may well read through this chapter making sure I do not say anything that contradicts earlier chapters! Or perhaps you simply want to know what I am saying to your children in preparation. Either way, enjoy.

If you are reading this as a child of a Baby Boomer +, welcome to a chapter designed for you. You likely did not buy the book for this one chapter but began perusing it at the bookstore as a gift for your parents or when you picked it up from the coffee table of your parents' home.

Having been in your shoes, as have your parents, though it might be hard to believe, I can't say enough about how your time and presence in your family matters on behalf of your parents' later years. You may, in fact, be right in the mix of having parents of the Baby Boomer + generation, your own life fast approaching time for your own later years planning, and still raising semi-younger children at home or in university. It's big.

This is a time to, as is so often called in the coaching world, play full out, the exact same words I used with your parents about designing their lives and talking with you about it. Just as it is easy for older adults to want to put off the conversation, the same is true for their adult children . . . and for the same reasons (*there's always tomorrow*), not wanting to have to face acknowledgement of the full circle of life with those you love. Additionally, perhaps you don't feel ready to participate in the responsibility yet, or in some cases, take the lead. However, as I say to your parents throughout these pages, engaging rather than avoiding will bring life-giving moments and peace of mind. You will navigate the coming years more fully in the flow of grace, energy, and compassion because you have chosen to be as prepared as possible. This brings far more ease than you might know in the moment. Trust me, it does. You will breathe and experience a grateful spirit.

There are two paths to this life-giving conversation and I want to speak to each one separately, though there is certainly overlap.

The path that is your parents' initiation

This is, of course, my WHY for writing this book, and it is my hope that 90% of the conversations that happen stem from my generation stepping into the courage and beauty to ask you, the children, to engage. For some, this is an easy request because your family talks about everything so of course you are happy to talk about the entirety of life and its closure. For many, however, the "ugh" comes up, both in the actual step over the threshold on the part of your parents to ask, and for you to step up to meet them rather than backing away. Layers and layers of family stories and history influence the feelings and the willingness for both to say yes.

When you say, "Yes, I count it a privilege for us to speak about this together," the life-giving aspect is mutual and doubled. If you feel resistance and create reasons to not have the conversation "yet," I encourage you to spend time reflecting on your own "why not?" What is it that is keeping you from stepping into this opportunity?

Let me offer some possible reasons that may or may not resonate:

- You cannot imagine your parents dying and to that end, you do not even know how to enter into that conversation, how to have it be "real"

- You are concerned about their choices for how they want to live these years and you do not know how to talk about that in a way that does not cause discomfort

- It will raise your own level of angst . . . period

- You believe that when your family comes together there will be either minor or full-blown differences of opinion that might hurt people's feelings and cause a rift . . . better to let things just be as they are . . . that can't hurt . . . and deal with each piece as it comes up

- This pulls you into a level of responsibility that is a new layer in the relationship

- Your parents ask for your approval or blessing, which has not been their MO so it feels awkward and new

All of the above reasons are completely understandable. There are many feelings connected to them.

At the same time, I want to find or create new, made-up, crazy strong words of encouragement to say do not let this pass you by. For whatever awkwardness or discomfort of facing reality, I cannot tell you how happy you will be when in the most important moments, you hold the keys (sometimes literally) of preparation rather than looking all over for clues as to how to find what you need. Thinking about the latter makes me cringe. It makes me want to sit with you over a cup of coffee and coach you around what is so much better . . . and to visualize the day you say *thank you, thank you, thank you* for the gift you were given.

Please do not let this opportunity pass you by. It is, as I have said in earlier pages, also setting a new paradigm, a new way of being as a family that you can pass on to your children and they can pass on to their children.

I invite you to say, "Yes, of course" on the first ask. Know that there are multiple moments of opportunity to explore so much about this time of life that your parents are relishing . . . relish it with and for them.

The path of your proactive initiation

It may be that for all the examples of reasons not to have the conversation that I list above, your parents have been completely silent. Perhaps they are staunchly independent and don't talk over anything with family or are of a mind that resists rocking the boat. Whatever the reason, you are living in total mystery about anything and everything concerning their current decisions and what they want at the end of their lives. You have no idea about finances. You are completely in the dark about whether they have created a will and if so, who the contact person is. You wonder if you will be able to find keys to the safe deposit box they occasionally mention. There may also be, if like mine, a plethora of passwords you could not possibly decipher on your own.

As much as you, too, would love to ignore the whole matter, there is a piece of you that wants very much to know the plan, to rest in the assurance that your life will not be turned upside down by confronting a chaotic or complex mess, to be quite honest. That—and worse—is how people describe what life is like when there has not been the life-giving conversation. Untold heartache, frustration, and time sucks can be completely avoided. They really can. Even if your parents have not come to you, you have the privilege of going to them and being the one to step over the threshold first to ask for the chat. You get to invite them to meet you in "yes." You are being responsibly proactive on behalf of all of you to bring this up and into the open, and you can look back through the chapters in Part II to help steer the way in which you get together.

It may also be that you sense one or both parents are shifting into more forgetfulness or encountering a physical condition that is taking a significant toll on energy; perhaps they are finding themselves incapable of thinking about or trying to bring family together to confront what can be a paradoxical hard truth and peacefulness.

In the conversations with my daughter it is not about the specifics of "inheritance." That is actually quite distant from my mind as I write because in many cases we cannot even know exactly what that will be. It is all about honoring, respecting, and knowing the most important details for what needs to be accessed when the time comes and how older adults want to embrace life now. Many shy away from the conversation for reasons of not being clear on "inheritance" details so I encourage that piece, which is what can too often become a rocky road between siblings, to be put aside for the sake of coming together in support.

Two things are crossing my mind as I type . . . for that is how I write; like life itself, it is not all planned-out. One is that this strikes me as the same age-old kind of conversation about how to tell kids about sex . . . "the talk" that either was or wasn't had. Now we're changing the topic, and "the talk" about life and death . . . celebrating both even before death happens and the circle of life is complete.

Randomly, or perhaps for good reason, the song "You Raise Me Up" by Josh Groban also comes into my head in this moment of writing . . . This conversation, no matter who initiates it, is one of raising each other up. Here are some of the lyrics:

When I am down, and, oh, my soul, so weary
When troubles come, and my heart burdened be
Then, I am still and wait here in the silence
Until you come and sit awhile with me

You raise me up, so I can stand on mountains
You raise me up to walk on stormy seas
I am strong when I am on your shoulders
You raise me up to more than I can be

It may be that those words fit. And even if the first part doesn't, even if everyone is in great energy together, the second part is a beautiful way to think about how you can all be in this conversation and life together. You might have other music and lyrics that come into your head based on what you know about your family. Go for it. Include them, too. Perhaps they inspire you and/or can be part of the celebration.

Whether approached or being the one who approaches, be willing and yes, I'll even dare say excited, to gather and talk and listen and support and know and be at ease and sleep well. All of it is possible even with potential bumps along the way. The worth, the high value, far surpasses any doubts and hesitations.

Email me if you have questions or thoughts. My contact information is at the back of the book and I'd love to hear from you. For me, this circles back to when my own parents asked us to gather by the barn that summer day and the circle comes around to my asking my daughter to sit with me . . .

bringing light into one another's lives in our presence and being centered together around what is a natural part of the circle of life.

MY PERSONAL INTENTION

For my daughter

The Dedication at the beginning of this book is to everyone, really, current Baby Boomers + and all generations after mine.

My intention has you at its center.

In this moment, on this last "real page," the book falls away, along with all that might come as a result of the writing falls away, even as I dream about speaking and holding seminars through which to share this work and be in life-giving conversation with others.

I now know, as I complete this call I followed, that in so many ways I wrote the book for myself, and by extension for me in relationship to you.

There is no person more important in my life.

The years are flying by like cars on amusement rides I watched at a fair this summer . . . dizzyingly fast . . . and while I am aiming for 100, I become more sensitively aware all the time that any time, any day could be a last day.

My intention is clear, just like "On a Clear Day." I will be the designer of my life for as long as possible, as I have always wanted you to be the designer of yours. One of the gifts of our relationship is that while we draw on each other as desired or needed, we live from our own convictions and decisions. There is tremendous freedom in that. Even as you confidently walked away from me without a glance back when going to Kindergarten and I felt a tug of "Wait!" I have always admired that your independent spirit showed up when you did at 2:44 PM all those years ago.

My intention is that you will be free of having to worry about me or care for me in any way for as long as possible. The only, and I do mean only regret I have about having an only child, is that if and when the time comes for more significant care, you do not have a sibling or two with whom to share that. That is something that has been on my mind for years.

This concern deepens my intention to share with you face to face and in joy how I choose to live these years, my hopes and dreams, and then add in all the additional details that will ease your life when the time comes for mine to conclude. We will decide how to celebrate the knowing of that and the transparency together. It is not an easy conversation to think about and makes me teary just to say it here. You know I have always been the teary one so we'll celebrate that too.

I am going to live *now* beautifully and make certain you get to send me off free of, "Wait, wait . . . you didn't tell me where_____ or what_____?"

My love for you is forever. Thank you for coming into this world to be my daughter.

RESOURCES

This book is a personal essay or I might even say an extremely lengthy letter to you that comes from my heart. It has not been written surrounded by research or a multitude of books on my desk. It has been written as if you and I were sitting having coffee together, simply sharing my thoughts, observations and intuition. That means there are not significant resources to share that have been specifically noted. However, I do want to mention a few specific books that may be interesting to read for this time in your life. A rather random collection, some of the books noted have no specific connection to Baby Boomers +. They are books I have enjoyed regardless of age. Some will appeal and some will not, as it is with all books!

I rarely choose a piece of non-fiction unless I feel it will be pertinent to me, so most always explore it before buying. I encourage you to do the same with the books mentioned here and to search for others that touch your heart and soul and give breadth and depth to these important pieces of life. There are also wonderful spiritual resources from myriad faith traditions, which I have purposely not included here for those are so personal. I imagine that there are also podcasts and TED talks and so much more. This short list barely scratches the surface of all that is available. And of course, if you are more of an auditory learner or travel frequently, audio books are terrific. Enjoy whatever it is you choose!

I would consider it a privilege to privately coach you and/or your family through this process. A person who is not as close to the family dynamic is an invaluable resource and can help neutralize the potential intensity of emotions and thoughts.

Bateson, Mary Catherine – *Composing a Further Life: The Age of Active Wisdom*

RESOURCES

Bridges, William – *Transitions: Making Sense of Life's Changes*

Brene Brown – *The Gifts of Imperfection: Let Go of Who You Think You're Supposed to Be and Embrace Who You Are*

Daring Greatly: How Courage to Be Vulnerable Transforms the Way We Live, Love, Parent and Lead

Rising Strong: The Reckoning, the Rumble, and the Revolution

Crowley, Chris & Lodge, Henry S., M.D. – *Younger Next Year for Women: Live Strong, Fit, and Sexy Until You're 80 and Beyond*

Younger Next Year: Live Strong, Fit and Sexy Until You're 80 and Beyond

Dweck, Carol – *Mindset: How We Can Learn to Fulfill Our Potential*

Fox, Jenifer M.Ed. – *Your Child's Strengths: Discover Them, Develop Them, Use Them*

Gawande, Atul – *Being Mortal: Medicine and What Matters in the End*

Groban, Josh – "You Raise Me Up"

L'Engle, Madeleine – *Walking on Water: Reflections on Faith and Art*

Leider, Richard J. and Webber, Alan M. – *Life Reimagined: Discovering Your New Life Possibilities*

Levov, Greg – *Callings: Finding and Following an Authentic Life*

Lightfoot, Sarah Lawrence – *The Third Chapter: Passion, Risk, and Adventure in the 25 Years After 50*

Nepo, Mark – *Seven Thousand Ways to Listen: Staying Close to What is Sacred*

Oliver, Mary – "When Death Comes"

O'Leary, John – *On Fire: The 7 Choices to Design a Radically Inspired Life*

Palmer, Parker – *Let Your Life Speak: Listening for the Choice of Vocation*

RESOURCES

Poo, Ai-Jen – *The Age of Dignity: Preparing for the Elder Boom in a Changing America*

Sincero, Jen – *You Are a Bad Ass: How to Stop Doubting Your Greatness and Start Living an Authentic Life*

Ruiz, Miguel – *The Four Agreements*

Sinek, Simon – *Start with Why: How Great Leaders Inspire Everyone to Take Action*

Stone, Douglas; Patton, Bruce; Heen, Sheila – *Difficult Conversations: How to Discuss What Matters Most*

Zander, Rosamunde & Zander, Benjamin – *The Art of Possibility: Transforming Professional and Personal Life*

Zander, Rosamunde – *Pathways to Possibility: Transforming Our Relationship with Ourselves, Each Other and the World*

Because I have no legal expertise and want to be sure I am not misinterpreted or that I misrepresent anything legal, I choose not to include specific information about legal documents. I trust you will seek out professionals in your own city or state of residence such as Centers on Aging, Senior Centers, Eldercare Attorneys, Estate Attorneys, or Financial Advisors, for example, who can give you the best guidance.

Please visit my website www.dawnsullypile.com or contact me at dawn@dawnsullypile.com if you would like to explore the privilege of working together. There are myriad avenues for this work, including speaking and seminars to explore this topic in community.

Also, I would be honored, if the book has inspired you, if you would go to Amazon.com and leave a review so that this work can reach an even broader audience. Thank you.

ACKNOWLEDGEMENTS

In the spring of 2016 I was invited to join Lew Forbes, an advisor with Ameriprise Financial in Atlanta, for one of his presentations for clients and friends of clients about important life matters, not simply financial matters. Lew is a coach in his financial role whether he claims to be or not, but for the sake of this particular evening he focused on the legal information and documentation one needs to have in order so that when death comes all is in place that can be in place. His invitation was for me to follow his presentation about the legal aspects by speaking about the importance of communication regarding those matters with family and how to engage in that conversation together. That was the birthing moment of this book and a new passion of mine. Thank you, Lew, and may all of your worries about my own retirement years be put to rest by being the catalyst for this work! Lew has believed in me since meeting and this is a celebration of his encouragement.

Thank you to Jena Schwartz, my editor, whose writing is some of the most soul filled, no holding back, invitational writing I know. You definitely are The Promptress. You are also a fabulous editor, though I am not sure I had you edit this page and I might regret it. Knowing the quality of your work it was easy to click "Accept" by all of your suggestions and tweaks, as well as mulling your thoughtful questions. I am forever grateful. Having coffee with you and finally meeting you face to face still feels delightful and perhaps I can now breathe back into your writing group once again. Check out Jena's website at www.jenaschwartz.com.

To 99Designs and darbonville, the designer who created this cover that was my top choice from the beginning. Thank you to 99Designs for offering design contests that work so beautifully. I want to especially thank darbonville for working with me through multiple iterations to reach this fabulous final product. I present it with pride and joy. The website for 99Designs is www.99designs.com

To Jen Henderson of Wild Words Formatting, who quickly and with such ease formatted this book for Kindle and the paperback. You made that dance happen in a way that I would have only stumbled through for weeks. You allowed my shoulders to go back down. You are bookmarked in my files! Jen's website is www.wildwordsformatting.com

To friends who supported me and cheered me on through these months, making me realize I would totally let you (and me!) down if I did not have a book for you to order . . . thank you for your enormous faith and unwavering "you can do this" as well as prodding, "So Dawn, where is your book?" You kept me stepping forward.

To those confused as I first struggled to articulate this work so have not yet trusted that it was worth risking my speaking, here it is and I can't wait to speak for your organization! Believe me, I understand your wondering because I had not entirely pinned it down yet.

To those of all ages and backgrounds and beliefs around the world who inspire me daily in far more ways than I could ever list here and who put my brain on a continual joy ride of more ideas and thoughts than I will ever be able to get on paper, thank you. Inspiration is the root of all that is written.

To all the organizations through which I have taken courses and learned how to navigate these waters or writing and so much more, I value every penny spent and hope to earn them all back! For this round, I especially want to acknowledge Chandler Bolt's Self Publishing School—www.selfpubishingschool.com—and the exceptional community it is, to which I was led by Hal Elrod of The Miracle Morning. The Miracle Morning—www.miraclemorning.com—helped me find my way every single day and has for over three years.

The end

Live fully as the designer of your
life in peace, joy, love and light.

Made in the USA
Columbia, SC
28 November 2017